The Five Goal College Plan

A Strategic Plan That Will Help You:

❖ Graduate from College in 4 to 4.5 years with a B.A. or B.S.
❖ Become and Operate as a Self Manager and Leader
❖ Become and Operate as a Career Planner and Manager
❖ Choose the Right Career Field/Position and College Major
❖ Obtain a Good Job at Graduation in Your Chosen Field

The Five Goal College Plan

A Strategic Plan That Will Help You:

❖ Graduate from College in 4 to 4.5 years with a B.A. or B.S.
❖ Become and Operate as a Self-Manager and Leader
❖ Become and Operate as a Career Planner and Manager
❖ Choose the Right Career Field/Position and College Major
❖ Obtain a Good Job at Graduation in Your Chosen Field

Copyright Michigan 2019

Developed by Dr. Michael V. Mulligan, Career Management Consultant
CEO, Mulligan & Associates Inc.
A Career Management Consulting Firm That Has Helped Over 10,000
Individuals with Career Planning and Finding Work
Founded in 1985
www.mulliganassoc.com
847-981-5725

The Five Goal College Plan

A Strategic Plan That Will Help You:

- ❖ Graduate from College in 4 to 4.5 years with a B.A. or B.S.
- ❖ Become and Operate as a Self Manager and Leader
- ❖ Become and Operate as a Career Planner and Manager
- ❖ Choose the Right Career Field/Position and College Major
- ❖ Obtain a Good Job at Graduation in Your Chosen Field

Copyright ©–Mulligan 2016
Developed by Dr. Michael V. Mulligan, Career Management Consultant
CEO, Mulligan & Associates Inc.
A Career Management Consulting Firm That Has Helped Over 10,000
Individuals with Career Planning and Finding Work
Founded in 1983
www.mulliganassoc.com
847 981-5725

THE FIVE GOAL COLLEGE PLAN
MEETING THE CHALLENGES OF COLLEGE AND GRADUATING IN 4
OR 4.5 YEARS WITH A B.A. OR B.S. AND A JOB IN YOUR FIELD

iUniverse books may be ordered through booksellers or by contacting:

iUniverse
1663 Liberty Drive
Bloomington, IN 47403
www.iuniverse.com
1-800-Authors (1-800-288-4677)

ISBN: 978-1-5320-0893-1 (sc)
ISBN: 978-1-5320-0894-8 (e)

Print information available on the last page.

iUniverse rev. date: 10/04/2016

Preface

Meeting the Challenges of College and Graduating
with a B.A. or B.S. Degree in 4 to 4.5 Years with a Good Job
Will Mean a Major Return on Investment for You and Your Family

Ben Cassleman, who wrote an article in *the* **November 23, 2014** *Wall Street Journal,* **says:** *"A bachelor's degree remains by far the clearest path to the middle class or moving up the employment ladder.* Even today with the competition for jobs, recent graduates with a B.A. degree have lower rates of unemployment, higher earnings, and better career prospects than their less educated peers. The unemployment rate this year for those with a bachelor's degree was 4.1% versus 11% for those with only a high school diploma and 9.8% for those who started college and did not finish. Employed college graduates earned 37% more than college dropouts in 2014.

You should know that the rising cost of a college education is hitting one group especially hard and that is the millions of students who drop out of college without earning a degree. As more individuals than ever attend college, more are dropping out before they even don a cap and gown. This means millions of students are taking on the debt of college without getting the earnings boost that come from a degree. Without making a decent salary, dropouts are four times more likely to default on their student loans."

Lauren Asher, President of The Institute for College Access and Success
The Wall Street Journal, November 23, 2014 says:
"Graduating with a lot of debt can be daunting. Having a lot of debt and not graduating is even more daunting".

A 2014 study by the Institute for Higher Education Policy, a Washington D.C. Research Firm found that 58% of the 1.8 million borrowers whose loans began to be due in 2009 had not received a degree and some 59% of them were delinquent on their loans or had defaulted. The problem has worsen due to fewer job opportunities for less-educated workers. Students who don't graduate with some sort of credential or degree are the ones who are having the most problems in repaying their loan.

According to the **U.S. Department of Labor,** 34 million Americans over 25 years old have some college credits but haven't received a degree, a rate that has grown roughly 700,000 individuals over the past three years. Individuals who enter college need to do a better job of career and curriculum planning so they take advantage of their college education.

The purpose of this **book** is to help each student who starts college graduate on their time line (hopefully in 4 to 4.5 years) with less debt and move into the right career field and starting position. We have developed *The Five Goal College Plan* to help students graduate within a reasonable timeline and make their college investment pay off.

Something to Remember

Most young adults do not develop and execute personal growth plans and consequently leave their career and life direction up to chance. This book provides self assessments and a college and career planning and employment placement process that helps young adults focus on college goals that will maximize their education, and place them on the right career path with a good job.

Dr. William Muse

Former President of the University of Akron, Auburn University and East Carolina University. Business Dean at Appalachian State University, University of Nebraska at Omaha and Texas A&M University. Also served as Vice Chancellor for Academic Programs at Texas A&M. Presently serving as Director of the National Issues Forum Institute

The Five Goal College Plan

The *Plan* contains **five goals** you need to achieve in college to launch a successful career journey.

The **first goal** is for you to graduate with a B.A. or B.S. degree within 4 to 4.5 years. To do this, you need to understand the characteristics of the students who are mostly likely to drop out of college and the primary reasons why they drop out. Then you can develop and execute a smart graduation plan.

The **second goal** is to for you to assess and analyze yourself as a *self manager* and *leader* and become both. You will fill out three surveys, the *Self Management Competency Assessment Survey*, *The Mulligan Leadership Personality Profile* and *The Personal and Social Maturity Survey*. You will self score and analyze the results of each survey. You will then develop, execute and meet a plan that will help you grow in these areas each year while in college.

To operate as a self manager and leader, you must:

- Take charge of your own life and become less dependent on others for direction.
- Be a self starter-visualize what you need to do each day and do it.
- Develop your personal and social competence or maturity
- Think and make decisions that are right for the moment and situation.
- Learn how to find the right people in the areas where you need help and advice.
- Establish boundaries with parents, friends, roommates and controlling people.
- Write daily, weekly, monthly and yearly objectives and complete tasks to meet the objectives.
- Chart a career path that is right for you and be able to obtain positions that advance a career.
- Place yourself in career positions that pay enough so you don't have to live at home.
- Be able to work alone and meet the expectations of your boss and others
- Anticipate and manage the changes you will face in adulthood and on the job.
- Develop a sound educational, career, financial, spiritual, mental and physical base so you are self sufficient and capable of helping others in the world.

The **third goal** is for you to assess and analyze yourself as a *career planner*. You will fill out the *Career Planning Assessment* which contains 100 items, self score it, analyze your results and work toward being a *career planne*r. You will review the *Route 56 Career Management Model* and *15 Career Advancement Strategies* and use this information to both plan and manage your career.

The **fourth goal** is for you to select a career field and take academic programs (undergraduate courses, graduate or professional school, certifications etc.) that will help you enter your chosen occupation.. You should keep in mind that there are over 20,000 job titles in the *Dictionary of Occupational Titles*. We would like you to think of one job title for yourself and that is **helper**. You want to put yourself in a career where you can help others in some way whether this is in a professional role (doctor, lawyer, dentist, teacher, CPA or tradesman) or helping an organization service or make product for the public.

The **fifth goal** of this *book* is to help you create and execute a *preparation plan* each year that will help you obtain the right position in your chosen field either before or right after you graduate.

In conclusion, if these five goals are met, you will become and operate as a self manager and career planner and manager and graduate on your time line with a good job in your field.

Michael V. Mulligan, Ph. D.

Table of Contents

Page...

1   **Goal One-** Graduate from College in 4 or 4.5 years with a B.A. or B.S degree. This Means Knowing Why Students Drop Out and Developing and Executing a Smart Graduation Plan.

2   **Task One-** Learn the Facts on College Student Dropouts

3   **Task Two** – Understand the Characteristics of Those Who Drop Out of College and the Six Major Reasons for Dropping Out and Develop a Plan with Solutions so You Don't Drop Out

8   **Task Three-** Review the Action Steps That You Should Take Each Year to Succeed in College

12 **Task Four–** Operate as "a Finder" on Campus so You Graduate on Your Target Date

14 **Task Five-** Continually Fill Out the *Route 66 College Satisfaction Survey* and Correct the Issues that Impact or Bother You.

16 **Task Six-** Develop a Strategic Graduation Plan and Execute and Meet the Plan

23 **Goal # Two** – *Assess and Analyze Yourself as a Self Manager and Leader and Develop, Execute and Achieve a Growth Plan to Become Both*

24 **Task One-**Fill Out the *Self Management Competency Survey*, Self Score It and Analyze Your Results Identifying Where You Need to Improve

28 **Task Two** –Fill Out the *Mulligan Leadership Personality Profile*, Self Score It and Identify Where You Need to Make Behavioral Changes to Succeed

48 **Task Three-**Fill Out the *Personal and Social Maturity Survey,* Self Score It and Identify Where You Need to Make Changes to Succeed

53 **Task Four-**Analyze What Your Parents Do for You and What You Do for Yourself and Develop a *Partnership Expectation PAC* with Them so You Become a Self Manager Sooner than Later

55 **Task Five-** Anticipate the Changes You will Face in College, Work and Life and Operate as a Self Manager.

58 **Goal # Three–**Assess and Analyze Yourself as a Career Planner and Identify Where You Need to Grow to be a Competent Career Planner

59 **Task One-** Fill out the *Career Planning Assessment,* Self Score It, Analyze Your Results and Identify Where You Need Coaching

72 **Task Two-** Learn the *Route 56 Career Management Model* Which Can Help You Manage Your Career from College to Retirement

77 **Task Three-**Review the *15 Proven Career Strategies* and Execute These Strategies as You Manage Your Career Journey

83 **Task Four-** Develop, Execute and Meet a Growth Plan to Become a Career Planner and Manager

Table of Contents Continued

Page

85   **Goal # Four-**_Understand Career Pathing, Yourself and the World of Work and Tentatively Select a Career Field/Path/Position and College Major to Pursue_

86   **Task One-** Understand the Definitions of Career Path, Career Field and Career Position

90   **Task Two-** Understand Why There is No Job Security Today

94   **Task Three-**Write Out Your Career Aspiration

96   **Task Four-** Understand Yourself- Rank Four Work Tasks and Relate Them to 26 Career Areas

97   **Task Five-** Understand Yourself- Rate Your Strengths on 100 Skills

101   **Task Six-** Understand the World of Work-Review the 10 Groups of Industries Listed in the _Expanded Occupational Outlook Handbook_

109   **Task Seven-**Understand the World of Work-Review the 115 Top Projected Career Positions until 2015 and Select Several That Appeal to You

112   **Task Eight-**Understand the World of Work- Review the Majors Offered by Colleges and Universities and Select Several That Appeal to You.

116   **Task Nine-** Understand the World of Work-Prepare Yourself to Conduct Exploratory and Informational Interviews to Gain Information on Organizations, Industries and People

119   **Task Ten-** Understand the World of Work- Learn about the Job Opportunities for College Graduates

122   **Task Eleven–** Create a _Career Profile_ from the Information Accumulated and Select a Tentative Career Field/Path and Major

126   **Goal Five** – _Develop and Execute a Preparation Plan so You Obtain a Good Job Just Before or Right After Graduation_

127   **Task One** – Select a Tentative Career Field/Path and Major and Take the Courses That Will Best Help You Launch Your Career Journey

133   **Task Two-**Know the Challenges Facing You after Graduation so You Can Use Your College Education to Prepare for Them

135   **Task Three** – Develop a Plan on What You are Going to do During the College Years to Build a Resume that will Land You a Job at Graduation

136   **Task Four** – Develop a Job Search Plan and Implement It Starting Your Freshman Year so You Obtain Interviews and a Good Job Offer at Graduation

148   **Task Five–** Identify the Work Factors that are Most Important to You

149   **Task Six-** Develop Your Interviewing and Negotiating Skills so You Obtain Job Offers that are the Right Fit

155   **Task Seven-**Review What the Professionals Say about Advancing Your Career

159   **Appendix A-** Sample Resumes

185   **Appendix B-** Sample Letters

202   **Appendix C-** 105 Fastest Growing Franchises in America

206   **Appendix D-** Bibliography

207   **Poem-**_The Person Who Wins is the Person Who Thinks He/She Can._

Something to Remember

Man Lives to Grow.
Man Grows by Acquiring Skills, Knowledge and Experience
And Putting What He/She Learns into Action

Dr. Robert R. Carkhuff

Goal # One
Develop a Plan to Graduate from College in 4 or 4.5 years with a B.A degree

Your **Plan** consists of completing the following *six tasks* your freshman year and continuing to complete tasks *two through six* each year in college until you graduate in 4 or 4.5 years or on your targeted date. The *six tasks* are the following:

Page

2   **Task One-** Learn the Facts about College Student Dropouts

3   **Task Two-** Understand the Characteristics of Those Who Drop Out of College and the Six Major Reasons for Dropping Out and Develop a Plan with Solutions so You Don't Drop Out.

8   **Task Three-** Review the Action Steps That You Should Take Each Year to Succeed in College

12   **Task Four-** Operate as "a Finder" on Campus so You Graduate on Your Target Date

14   **Task Five-** Continually Fill Out the *Route 66 College Satisfaction Survey* and Correct the Issues that Impact or Bother You.

16   **Task Six-** Develop a Strategic Graduation Plan and Execute and Meet the Plan.

Task One
Learn the Facts about College Student Dropouts

Dr. Wesley R. Habley[1], Principal Associate, Educational Services of the *American College Testing Program* did a study with Jennifer Bloom and Steve Robbins in 2014 on *Student Graduation Trends from 1983 to 2014.* Their findings are outlined below.

Student Graduation Trends from 1983 to 2014
Percentage of Students Attending Two Year Colleges That Graduated in Three Years or Less

	Highest % Year	Lowest % Year	Current % Year
Two Year Public	38.8% (1989)	25.4% (2012)	25.4% (2014)
Two Year Private	66.4% (1990)	50.2% (1998)	51.4% (2014)
All Two Year	44.0 (1989)	28.3% (2010)	29.1% (2014)

- The data shows that more students in 1989 and 1990 graduated within three years than those attending a two year college in 2012 and 2014..
- 25% of students attending a public two year college in 2014 graduate within three years.
- 51% of students attending a private two year college in 2014 graduate within three years.

Percentage of Students Attending a Four Year Public or Private College That Graduated in Five Years or Less

	Highest% Year	Lowest % Year	Current % Year
B.A/B.S. Public	52.8% (1986)	36.6% (2010)	36.6% (2014)
M.A/M.S. Public	46.7% (1986)	37.0% (2000)	38.3% (2014)
Ph.D. Public	50.6% (1989 & 90)	45.0% (2001)	48.0% (2014)
B.A/B.S. Private	57.5% (2006)	53.3% (2001)	54.7% (2014)
M.A/M.S. Private	58.4% (1988)	53.5% (2001)	55.7% (2014)
Ph.D. Private	68.8% (1986)	62.9% 2012)	62.9% (2014)

- The data shows that more students attending private and public four year colleges and universities in the late 80's graduated within five years than students in 2014.
- **48%** of students who attend *public universities* offering a Ph.D. program, **38.3%** who attend a M.A./M.S. *public university* and **36.6%** enrolled at a *four year public college* offering a B.A. or B.S. graduated within five years or less.
- **62.9%** of students who attend *private universities* offering a Ph.D. program, **55.7%** who attend a M.A./M.S. *private institution* and **36.6%** enrolled at a *four year private college* offering a B.A. or B.S. graduated within five years or less.

The bottom line is that *less than half* of the students attending a two year college graduate in three years and about *half* attending a four year college/university graduate within five years.

John Gardner, a researcher says: "That in spite all we know about student retention, college faculty and administrators are still inclined to hold students more accountable for graduating than themselves. This is why we developed *The Five Goal College Plan* for you, the student.

<u>Task Two</u>

Understand the Characteristics of Those Dropping Out and the Six Major Reasons Why Students Drop Out of College and Develop a Plan/Solutions

Those Who are Most Likely to Drop Out of College are Students:
- with low academic achievement; students not ready for college
- with limited education aspirations; not motivated to put in the necessary work
- who are indecisive about a major/career goal; lack career direction and purpose
- with inadequate financial resources; can't afford to attend college
- who are economically disadvantaged; operating in a new culture
- who are the first generation students; no one to guide them at home
- who are commuters; facing many challenges at home and college at the same time
- who are non self managers- not organized & susceptible to alcohol/drugs/ parties

The *Six Major Reasons* Why Students Leave College are:
- poor academic planning
- unprepared academically
- lack of certainty about major/career
- transition/adjustment difficulties
- dissonance/incompatibility with the people and policies of the campus
- irrelevancy and cost – What am I getting for my money? (Noel & Levitz, 2010)[2]

Let's discuss these six reasons and identify some solutions that can help you succeed.

1). Poor Academic Planning –Taking the right courses

<u>Causes-</u> There are a number of reasons for poor academic planning

- You have not written out the courses you need to take to graduate.
- No one reviewed your test scores & H.S. courses before assigning you classes.
- You are signing up for courses just to fill your schedule.. There is no relevance between the courses you are taking and your academic major and direction.

<u>A Plan-Solutions</u>
- Make sure the college reviews your AP scores if you took Advanced Placement courses in high school. Also, a 25 score or higher on each of the ACT tests of educational development should qualify you to take departmental exams on campus that can exempt you from a college course or give you credit.
- If you don't have an academic advisor who is knowledgeable about you and the courses you should take, seek out someone on the faculty who can help you. Don't let one academic advisor build a "failure or boring "program for you. Explore taking challenging and relevant courses outside your major that can enhance your chances of obtaining a job after graduation.

3

2. **Unprepared Academically**

Causes

The basic reason for high school students not being ready academically for college is that they don't take the proper courses in high school. High School students don't read enough and usually register for the easy courses in high school so they can make an A.

The American College Testing Program[3] has completed many studies with colleges and universities across the United States and have developed college readiness benchmark scores to connect college readiness to the college classroom. A benchmark score is the minimum score needed on an ACT subject-area test to indicate 50% chance of obtaining a B grade or higher or about a 75% chance of obtaining a C or higher in the corresponding credit-bearing college course. The College Readiness Benchmark Scores for English Composition, Algebra, Social Science and Biology are below.

College Course/Course Area	ACT Test	Benchmark Score
English Composition	English	18
Algebra	Mathematics	22
Social Science	Reading	21
Biology	Science	24

The 2015 National ACT Report which included 1,666,017 test takers, revealed the following statistics in regard to developmental consideration for students:

- In 2015, 67% of the test takers scored an *18* or higher on the ACT English Test which means 33% of the test takers need tutoring or to take a remedial class.
- In 2015, 46% of the test takers scored a *22* or higher on the ACT Math Test which means 54% of the test takers need tutoring or to take a remedial class.
- In 2015, 52% of the test takers scored a 21 or higher on the ACT Reading Test which means 48% need tutoring or to take a remedial course.
- In 2015, 31% of the test takers scored a 24 or higher on the ACT Science Test which means 69% need tutoring or to take a remedial course.
- In 2015, 27% of the test takers made test scores that matched all four benchmarks of the four ACT tests of educational development. This means 73% of the test takers did not meet all four test benchmarks set by the American College Testing Program.

A Plan-Solutions

1. Be sure you know your strengths and weaknesses in math, science, English and reading. If you are weak in any one area, find help. Take a remedial course or find a private tutor.
2. Be sure not to take all the hard courses your freshmen year meaning courses where you are weak academically. Develop a strategy so you balance the hard and easier courses so you can make a satisfactory grade point average.
3. You should attend class regularly and take good notes. Take a course on how to study and organize your time.

4. Learn the teaching style of your instructor and what he or she expects.
5. If you don't learn something in a class, attend the class again the same day. Review the subject matter on line and talk to your peers who are in the class.
6. Study in groups and review the material together before class.

3. Uncertainty of Major and Career Goal

Causes

The world of work is very complex. Community Colleges will offer both a transfer program to four year colleges and universities plus one or two year career related programs. Liberal Arts Colleges will offer 15 to 30 majors and universities will offer as many as 180 majors. There are over 22,000 occupations and 90 types of industries from which to choose. The problem is that we don't know enough about ourselves and the world of work to make a good decision. They say only 8 % of the students go into a career that is related to their college major so it might not be a good thing for you to spend six years trying to get all the courses for a major that will not produce employment or a career path.

A Plan-Solutions

- Review some of the career related courses that two year colleges offer. Maybe you might find a program that fits you and gets you started in a career earlier.
- Visit the counseling center to take assessments and receive career counseling.
- Fill out the *Career Development Needs Assessment* in this book and learn what you know and don't know about planning and managing your career journey.
- Meet *Goals 4* (Select a Career Field and Major) and *5* (Obtain a Job) in this book.
- Take internships in the career field and with the organizations that you like. The organization might hire you full time after you graduate..
- Work as a co-op student while attending college if you don't have money saved for college. It pays for your college education while you learn about a career field.
- It is best to finish college in four years and use the money you would spend on your fifth year to obtain your masters in a special area. Research shows that eight out of ten college graduates are normally working in an area that is not related directly to their major. Therefore, students should major in an area they like, can pass and graduate sooner.
- One of the best ways to prepare for a career field and position is to attend college and study a specific curriculum that is related to your career goal. However, many think a liberal arts curriculum will make you well rounded and you can specialize later. We have had employers tell us that liberal arts students make good salespeople and executives.
- A student should realize obtaining the undergraduate B.A. degree is important. It opens the door for higher level employment and graduate and professional school. Most people move into a career based on opportunities at work or going on to graduate or professional school. You should also take relevant courses in other areas than your major.
- You might discover taking a few elective courses could lead you in a new career direction. A course or two in computers and business can help you get an interview in the business world even if you are majoring in an unrelated field. You can obtain a license to sell real estate by passing one course and the state examination.

- Many fields require completion of only a one, two, or three-year program. Many students go back to school to complete these programs after they complete their B.A. degree.
- Many students who graduate with a B.A. or B.S. in liberal-arts can specialize in certain career areas later by obtaining a master's degree or by completing a special training program in their company.
- Your chances of moving up the career ladder in the world of work can increase with additional education. Many colleges in the country offer an MBA or masters program in many areas so check out these programs.
- Continued education and padding your credentials is an effective way to keep your position and be competitive in the job market.

4.. Adjustment Difficulties

Students who are away from home for the first time have a lot of adjustments to make. It is a new environment and there is a lot to learn, plus new people to meet. All of these new experiences can become overwhelming. Those who commute will still have demands made on them at home as well as at college.

The National Center on Alcohol and Substance Abuse[4] states that 3.8 million college students binge drink or take drugs every year. A study from 1993 to 2010 revealed that 49% of college students binge drink or take drugs. Over 1,717 college students died in 2009 because of alcohol or drugs. This report was revealed on the Lou Dobbs CNN show March 20.2014.

A Plan-Solutions

- You should find an effective academic advisor, an upper classman who will serve as a mentor, and develop some friendships early for support.
- You should get to know your R.A. in your residence hall and seek help when needed.
- Be smart about the number of activities you involve yourself in on campus. One might pledge a fraternity while playing a varsity sport or participating in an activity that takes a lot of time. You should give yourself time to study so you can make good grades.
- Learn how to establish boundaries with your roommate, friends and your parents. There have been reports some parents might talk to their college students over six times a day.
- Organize your time so you have time to study whether you live at college or at home.
- You want to control your drinking and not take drugs on campus. The peer pressure to drink and take drugs can be great. Your health is more important than being liked. The opportunity to attend college is a privilege and students shouldn't blow this honor by getting carried away with drinking and drugs. Don't let the weekends of drinking take over your academic week in college.
- If you suffer from depression, an eating disorder or something that can impact your ability to function at college, seek out help and set up a structured situation for yourself with a campus official or a professional locally.

5. Dissonance or Incompatibility

Cause

You are always going to find people who are different from you. Part of your college experience is to learn how to get along with a variety of people and know how to react in certain situations.

A Plan-Solutions

- Join groups that have similar interests with you but try a diversified group.
- If certain people impact you in a negative manner, like your roommate or academic advisor, talk to them and try to make adjustments. If it can't be worked out, remove yourself from the situation. Don't wait until it hurts you academically or emotionally. Talk to someone on campus who can help you.
- Fill out the *Route 66 College Satisfaction Survey* in *Task Five* of this section once and a while and discover how you like the college you are attending. Work on those things that bother you. In other words, identify what you don't like about your college situation and do something about it.

6. Irrelevancy and Cost to Attend College

Cause

We do things for a reason. If the reason doesn't make sense to us and it is costing us a lot of money, we aren't as committed to college. It impacts our motivation in a negative way.

A Plan-Solutions

- You should select a tentative career field and take the curriculum at your college that best prepares you for that field. You can also take a few relevant courses elsewhere.
- You should talk to people in the occupation and industry that appeals to you. Ask these individuals what courses are important to take.
- If you feel some of your courses are irrelevant, talk to your professor so you can work together to make the experience a positive one.
- Know the importance of obtaining a college degree. You need to understand how a college education can help you move up the social/economic ladder of life. Listed below is the lifetime income based on level of education:

Lifetime Income

High School Diploma	$1,100,000
Bachelor's Degree	$2,100,000
Masters Degree	$2,500,000
Doctorate Degree	$4,400,000

(Source: Dr. Phil Gardner, *2014 Recruiting Trends Report*, Michigan State University[5])

Task Three-
Review the Action Steps That You Should
Take Each Year to Succeed in College

As a freshman student, you should:

1) Learn if you qualify and then take departmental exams to exempt freshmen academic core courses (English, math, science, social studies and a foreign language) to obtain academic credit.
2) Learn if your AP scores from High School Advance Placement Courses will gain you college credit.
3) Find and work with an academic advisor who cares about you and will help schedule a class load that you can handle and make a C+ or better average.
4) Learn how to set priorities, organize your time and study properly.
5) Visit the career counseling center to take some assessments and talk with a career counselor about a career field and college major.
6) Complete the *Career Management Competency Survey* in this Guide and talk to the people who can help you become competent in the areas where you need to become competent.
7) Learn about the various courses on campus. If freshman have electives, you should take a couple of courses in your high interest area.
8) Go to the career center and learn how to write an effective resume. Your resume should be started the freshman year and developed through out the college years.
9) Learn about the organizations on campus that can best help you develop your leadership, management and people skills.
10) Start developing your job search network contact list on your computer. You should put the names of parents and alumni that you meet on a list with their career backgrounds, companies, addresses, phone numbers and emails.
11) Learn about internship programs and sign up for one that matches your targeted career field and positions.
12) Take the necessary academic load to be a sophomore in September of next year. If not, attend summer school at home or take on line courses.
13) Don't get involved in binge drinking or drugs where it takes over your life.
14) Take a foreign language so you are bilingual. Since the Hispanic population is one of the largest growing cultures in the USA, Spanish would pay off later or even Chinese.
15) Strive to be the best of the best in your class; fill leadership positions, participate in community and worldly affairs, and work on your interpersonal communication and human relations maturity.
16) Study more and spend less time on the cell phone, computer, texting, and Face Book.
17) Continue to improve yourself as a self manager and leader.
18) Continue to review the courses you need to take to graduate.

What other action steps do you need to take your freshman year to succeed?

As a sophomore student, you should:

1) Target a career field and select a major that will help you obtain a position in your chosen field.
2) Continue to fill leadership positions on campus and take internships that will help you. develop a strong resume and gain work experience in your chosen career field.
3) Continue to add names of parents and alumni to your job search computer networking list.
4) Strive to be classified a junior in September of next year and obtain a "B" average or better
5) Finish your second year of a foreign language.
6) Study more and spend less time texting, on the computer, cell phone and Face Book.
7) Not let others involve you in binge drinking and drugs.
8) Continue to review the courses you need to take to graduate.
What other action steps should you take to be successful in your sophomore year?

As a junior student, you should:

1). Enter your major study area and strive to make a "B" or better average in your major.
2). Continue to join relevant organizations and fill leadership positions on campus.
3). Take internships that are in their chosen career field. These experiences can be added to your resume and work experience.
4) Prepare yourself to conduct an effective job search.
5) Sharpen your telephone, networking and interviewing skills.

6) Don't get involved in binge drinking or drugs.

7) Organize a career advancement network group with students in the same major and pledge

8) Continue to add names to your job search computer networking list.

9) Conduct informational interviews with people in your chosen career field.

10) Make sure you are classified as a senior in September of the next year.

11) Know the courses you need to complete your senior year to graduate and if you can't get them on your campus, take the course(s) in summer school elsewhere if it is necessary to graduate on time.

What other action steps should you take to be successful in your junior year?

As a senior year student, you should:

1).Continue to be a leader on campus and add these accomplishments as well as work achievements to their resume.
2).Work with your career advancement network group to obtain interviews now and later.
3).Should start to contact people on their network computer list about possible positions in their company and elsewhere.
4).Strive to maintain a "B" or better average in their major and overall "B" average to be accepted into graduate and professional school.
5).Try to obtain as many interviews as possible and take the best job offer.
6).Work toward obtaining a good job offer before graduation so you can put yourself at ease and show your parents that good planning pays off.
7) Know the courses you need to complete your senior year to graduate
What other action steps should you take to be successful in your senior year?

As a fifth year student, you should:

1). Continue to be a leader on campus and add these accomplishments as well as work achievements to their resume.
2). Work with your career advancement network group of fellow majors to obtain interviews.
3). Should start to contact people on your network computer list about possible positions in their company and elsewhere.
4). Strive to maintain a "B" or better average in your major and overall to be accepted into graduate and professional school.
5). Try to obtain as many interviews as possible and take the best job offer.
6). Work toward obtaining a good job offer before graduation so you feel good about yourself and know that good planning pays off.
7) Know the courses you need to complete to graduate.
What other action steps should you take to be successful in your fifth year?

What Works in Student Retention (Habley and McClanahan, 2014)[6]. ACT conducted the 2014 year study, which can be found www.act.org/research/policymakers/reports/retain.html. When asked to identify the six campus retention practices that had the greatest impact on student retention, all survey respondents identified at least one of the following.

- Freshman seminar/university 101 for credit
- Tutoring program
- Advising interventions with selected student populations
- Mandated course placement testing program
- Comprehensive learning assistance center/lab
- One-On-One College Coaching-Having a college mentor on campus

What do you think your major impediments will be to graduating on your timeline and what are your solutions to overcoming each impediment?

Task Four-
Operate as "a Finder" on Campus so You Graduate on Your Target Date

One of the major characteristics of being a self manager is to be able to operate as a *finder*. You can't sit in your room and expect people on campus to come to you. In college, you must find:

- A professional in the financial aid office who will help you obtain financial aid and student work that will pay the college bills.
- An academic advisor who will help you schedule the right academic load each semester , number of hours to take and difficulty of courses and overall the courses needed to graduate on time.
- A counselor in the Career Services Center that will help you choose the right career field, college major and assist you in obtaining internships.
- Professors who have the reputation of being fair graders and going the extra mile to help students pass.
- A tutor to help you in subject matter that is difficult for you
- The courses that might be extremely difficult for you. You might take the same courses in the summer at a less competitive academic college. You can make a higher grade and this helps you build up your overall grade point average when applying for graduate or professional school later.
- Students in your class that would like to be part of a study group. The objective of the group is to help everyone pass the course with a good grade without cheating.
- A roommate who wants to make good grades and graduate on their target date.
- A place to study if you can't study in your room.
- A professional in the library who can show you how to use the library for class research and to conduct a job search later.
- A mentor in your chosen career field. It can be an alumnus, a friend of the family or a mentor from a company where you are doing an internship. They can help guide and coach you on how to find the right job.
- A small group of students in your major who want to help each other graduate and find a job before graduation. This group can be called The Career Advancement Networking Team and it can help everyone on the team advance in their career through out life.
- A way to work with your parents. You need to identify how your parents can work with you to find internships and launch a career that is right for you and not them.
- Parents of your friends on campus that can help you find an internship or job.
- A finance professional who can educate you on credit card debt and other financial planning matters.
- The individuals in companies or organizations that can offer you a job or position after you graduate.

Who did we leave off the list that you should have on it?

Make a List of Those People Who Can Help You When You Need Them

Task Five-
Continually Fill Out the *Route 66 College Satisfaction Survey* ©
During College and Correct the Issues that Impact or Bother You.

The purpose of this evaluation in to determine if you are on the right college route. We have developed a college route satisfaction evaluation system to determine if you are happy today with your college experience.

Right Fit – Are you satisfied with your college experience?

(You should answer yes if you are satisfied or no if you are dissatisfied with each of the following 10 statements)

Right Fit- Are You Satisfied?

1. The college or university did an excellent job of orienting me to the campus, introducing me to the people I should know on campus and helping me in the areas where I need help.
   _____ yes   _____ no
2. The college or university has done and continuously does a good job of helping me come up with a financial package to pay for my education.
   _____ yes   _____ no
3. The college or university did a good job of testing me for academic readiness and placing me in the right courses to start.
   _____ yes   _____ no
4. The college or university has done a good job in helping me select a college major and outlining the courses I need to take to graduate in the timeline I set for myself.
   _____ yes   _____ no
5. The academic advisor cares about me and has done a good job of helping me schedule my classes.
   _____ yes   _____ no
6. The professors know their subject matter, are good teachers and care about the students.
   _____ yes   _____ no
7. The students and faculty on campus are very friendly and make you feel like you belong.
   _____ yes   _____ no
8. I have had the opportunity to use and develop my talent on campus in various clubs, organizations, sports, and in the classroom.
   _____ yes   _____ no
9. The college or university has helped me with career planning, obtaining internships and part-time work, and will help me find a job after graduation.
   _____ yes   _____ no
10. The college or university has helped me grow and develop the skills that are necessary to be successful in a career and the world.
    _____ yes   _____ no

Add up the number of yes and no answers   _____Yes   _____No

Right Rewards – Are You Satisfied? ©

(Answer <u>yes</u> if you are satisfied or <u>no</u> if you are dissatisfied to each of the 10 statements)

1. I feel secure on campus.

     _____ yes   _____ no

2. I feel like I am part of our college nation..

     _____ yes   _____ no

3. I feel the professors, students and administration want me to succeed.

     _____ yes   _____ no

4. I feel constantly challenged and that I am meeting the challenges of college.

     _____ yes   _____ no

5. I feel my potential is being developed.

     _____ yes   _____ no

6. I feel like I am learning how to think for myself and make good decisions.

     _____ yes   _____ no

7. I feel like I am been exposed to the world and people of all backgrounds.

     _____ yes   _____ no

8. I feel I have developed skills that will help me in the world of work and life.

     _____ yes   _____ no

9. I feel I have developed a network of college friends that will be in touch with me forever.

     _____ yes   _____ no

10. I feel the college or university is doing and has done a great job of preparing me for a career and how to contribute to the world. The financial investment has been worth it.

     _____ yes   _____ no

What is your College Satisfaction Route Rating Score?

Right Fit _____ Did you answer yes six times or more?
(score – add up your **yes** answers from previous page-hopefully you have six or more)
Right Rewards _____ Did you answer yes six times or more?
(score – add up your **yes** answers from this page- hopefully you have six or more)

What College Satisfaction Route are You On? _____   _____

                                                   Right Fit Score   Right Rewards Score
You should be on the *College Satisfaction Route 66 or* higher or do something about moving your College Route Satisfaction Score Higher. Review your <u>No</u> answers and work on them.

Task Six
Develop a Timeline Graduation Plan and Execute and Meet the Plan

The number one reason why it takes some students more than three years to graduate from a community college and five years to graduate from a four year college or university is the **lack of career direction and poor academic/curriculum planning.** *Most students take more courses and hours than they need to take to graduate and this can be expensive.*

You need to find an academic advisor in your targeted career field area that cares about students. Set up an appointment to see him/her early in your freshman year. You should have a tentatively career field and major in mind and sit down with this advisor and identify the required courses you need to take and those electives you can take for credit that will help you meet the graduation requirements.

Please keep in mind that you are not required to graduate within three years at a two year college or within five years at a four year college or university. You can work a semester and go to school a semester or take a lighter load and work part time if you want to keep your loan debt down The challenge is completing all your courses with a C grade or better. Check and see if you receive credit for D grades. You don't want many of them. You also want to investigate what courses you can take online or at another college near your home that will substitute for some of the required courses at the college where you will receive your degree. You should become good friends with someone from the Registrar's office to know that you are on course to graduate.

Write Out Your College Status Below-Freshman, Sophomore, Junior or Senior

I am a _____ at a community college and plan to take a career program.
I am a _____ at a community college and plan to transfer to a four year college or university after I graduate.
I am a _____ at a community college and plan to transfer to a four year college or university when it is appropriate for me to do so.
I am a _____ at a four year college or university.

List below your starting date at your college and the date you expect to graduate.
*Starting Date*_____ *Graduation Date*_____
What is your targeted career field and major?_____
What degree will you obtain on your graduation date?_____

Make a list of the courses on the following pages that are required for your major and those that can serve as electives-courses which can go toward the number of hours you need to graduate. You might ask which courses on the list you could take at another college that would satisfy the academic requirement at the college you are now attending. Check off the courses as you complete them.

16

Required Courses-Freshman Year-100 & 200 Level Courses
Course Name   **# of Hours**

1. _____

2. _____

3. _____

4. _____

5. _____

6. _____

7. _____

8. _____

9 _____

10 _____

11 _____

12_____

Freshman Course Electives – 100 & 200 Level Courses
Course Name   **# of Hours**

13._____

14_____

15_____

16_____

17._____

18._____

19._____

20._____

Required Courses-Sophomore Year-100 and 200 Plus Level Courses
Course Name   # of Hours

1. _____

2. _____

3. _____

4. _____

5. _____

6. _____

7. _____

8. _____

9 _____

10. _____

11. _____

12. _____

Sophomore Course Electives – 100 and 200 Plus Level Courses
Course Name   # of Hours

13. _____

14 _____

15 _____

16 _____

17. _____

18. _____

19. _____

20. _____

Required Courses-Junior Year-200 Plus Level Courses
Course Name   **# of Hours**

1. _____

2. _____

3. _____

4. _____

5. _____

6. _____

7. _____

8. _____

9 _____

10. _____

11. _____

12. _____

Junior Course Electives – 200 Plus Level Courses
Course Name   **# of Hours**

13. _____

14 _____

15 _____

16 _____

17. _____

18. _____

19. _____

20. _____

Required Courses-Senior Year-200 Plus Level Courses

Course Name   **# of Hours**

1. _____

2. _____

3. _____

4. _____

5. _____

6. _____

7. _____

8. _____

9. _____

10. _____

11. _____

12. _____

Senior Course Electives – 200 Plus Level Courses

Course Name   **# of Hours**

13. _____

14. _____

15. _____

16. _____

17. _____

18. _____

19. _____

20. _____

Required Courses-Fifth Year-200 Plus Level Courses

Course Name   **# of Hours**

1. _____

2. _____

3. _____

4. _____

5. _____

6. _____

7. _____

8. _____

9. _____

10. _____

11. _____

12. _____

Fifth Year Course Electives – 200 Plus Level Courses

Course Name   **# of Hours**

13. _____

14 _____

15 _____

16 _____

17. _____

18. _____

19. _____

20. _____

Something to Remember

Becoming and operating as a self manager

is a very important step to performing tasks that are expected

of you in college, work and life.

Mike Mulligan Ph.D.
CEO Mulligan & Associates Inc.

Goal # Two –
Assess and Analyze Yourself as a Self Manager and Leader
And Develop, Execute and Achieve a Growth Plan

Page

24   **Task One**-Fill Out the *Self Management Competency Survey*, Self
       Score It and Analyze Your Results Identifying Where You Need to
       Improve as a Self Manager

28   **Task Two** –Fill Out the *Mulligan Leadership Personality Profile*,
       Self Score It and Analyze Your Results Identifying Where You Need to
       Make Behavioral Changes to Succeed

48   **Task Three**- Fill Out the *Personal and Social Maturity (E.Q.)*
       Survey, Self Score It and Identify Where You Need to Make Changes
       to Succeed

53   **Task Four**-Analyze What Your Parents Do for You and What You
       Do for Yourself and Develop a *Partnership Expectation PAC* with
       Them so You Become a Self Manager Sooner than Later

55   **Task Five**- Anticipate the Changes You will Face in College, Work and Life
       and Operate as a Self Manager

. Task One-
Fill Out the *Self Management Competency Survey*, Self Score It and
Analyze Your Results Identifying Where You Need to Improve

Listed below are 30 tasks that you should be capable and willing to do to operate as a self manager in life and college. You should record the appropriate number below that reflects your perception of your capability and willingness at this time to carry out certain self management tasks. After completing this assignment and evaluating yourself, identify six areas of the 30 that you need to improve on the most and develop a growth plan.

5 - Extremely capable and willing   (no developmental need)
4 – Above average in capability and willingness   (minimum developmental need)
3 - Average in capability and willingness   (moderate developmental need)
2 - Below average in capability and willingness   (a developmental need)
1 - Not very capable and willing   (a strong developmental need)

(Self Management Assessment Survey–

_____1. Capable and willing to take charge and direct my life without someone constantly telling me what to do.

_____2. Capable and willing to visualize what needs to be done each day and do it with enthusiasm and a positive attitude.

_____3. Capable and willing to make decisions that are right for the moment and situation.

_____4. Capable and willing to make daily, weekly, monthly and yearly objectives and persist to achieve them.

_____5 Capable and willing to understand and place myself in a position, situation and environment where I will more likely succeed than fail.

_____6 Capable and willing to discipline myself to compete in a performance measured environment without easily giving up.

_____7 Capable and willing to find the right people when I need advice and help.

_____8. Capable and willing to establish priorities and focus on them without being distracted by other people and situations-good time management.

_____9. Capable and willing to set boundaries with parents, friends, bosses, spouse, my own children and others.

_____10. Capable and willing to measure and develop my personal and social maturity so I can interact with people in a positive way.

_____11. Capable and willing to develop personal growth objectives and take action steps to achieve these objectives.

_____12. Capable and willing to accept the goals of others and work with them to meet the established goals.

_____13. Capable and willing to take on stressful work without losing my composure and focus on what needs to be accomplished.

_____14. Capable and willing to organize myself and complete the everyday tasks expected of me.

24

5 - Extremely capable and willing   (no developmental need)
4 –Above average in capability and willingness   (minimum developmental need)
3 - Average in capability and willingness   (moderate developmental need)
2 - Below average in capability and willingness   (a developmental need)
1 - Not very capable and willing   (a strong developmental need)

_____ 15. Capable and willing to display self discipline in spending money, taking care of my health, and getting things done.

_____ 16. Capable and willing to do the research and analyze situations more thoroughly when solving problems or making important decisions.

_____ 17. Capable and willing to work with my professors, bosses, peers, direct reports and people who come from a diverse background to meet goals.

_____ 18. Capable and willing to lead and follow others.

_____ 19. Capable and willing to take on the responsibility of adulthood, financial independence, and fatherhood and motherhood with the right person.

_____ 20. Capable and willing to meet my educational, career, financial, and spiritual base goals and be mentally , financially, physically and spiritually strong so I can help others in this world

_____ 21. Capable and willing to assess my academic strengths and weaknesses early in college so I can take the appropriate courses to move forward and succeed.

_____ 22. Capable and willing to improve my writing skills, math and science knowledge and reading speed and vocabulary.

_____ 23. Capable and willing to develop my leadership skills.

_____ 24. Capable and willing to develop my listening and responding skills.

_____ 25. Capable and willing to do the research and take courses that will help me in my career.

_____ 26. Capable and willing to keep up with the latest technology and social media so I can be an asset to campus clubs and organizations that employ me.

_____ 27. Capable and willing to organize myself so I can make it to class on time each day and graduate from college with the best grade point I can achieve.

_____ 28. Capable and willing to work with my professors keeping my home work and papers up to date so I can avoid stressful time limitations.

_____ 29. Capable and willing to be mature about drinking, smoking, taking drugs and driving my car texting or talking on the cell phone.

_____ 30. Capable and willing to take the steps to graduate on my designated date with a good job in my chosen field.

_____ **Total Points -*Self Management Score***

120 to 150 = A grade (Do not need counseling and coaching)
 90 to 119 = B grade (Need minimum amount of counseling and coaching)
 60 to 89 = C grade (Need moderate amount of counseling and coaching)
 30 to 59 =   D grade (Need counseling and coaching help)
 0 to 29 =   F grade   (Need lots of counseling and coaching)

Identify six tasks of the 30 where you need counseling and coaching or to take action to improve yourself. Write out your growth plan for each area.

<u>Task #One</u>

<u>Task # Two</u>

<u>Task # Three</u>

26

Task # Four

Task # Five

Task # Six

Task Two
Fill Out the *Mulligan Leadership Personality Profile,* ©
Self Score It and Identify Where You Need to Make Changes to Succeed

|Name _____

|Cell Phone# _____

Listed below are common phrases used to describe people. Read each phrase and evaluate the degree to which the phrase <u>describes you</u>. Please answer all 80 items marking the number that best describes you. Thank you.

(Scale)

6. This is <u>Definitely like</u> Me   5.This is <u>Usually like</u> Me   4. This is <u>Slightly like</u> Me

3. This is <u>Very Little like</u> Me   2. This is <u>Not like</u> Me   1.This is the <u>Opposite</u> of Me

1)	Self Starter-Get Things Done	6	5	4	3	2	1
2)	Don't Accept Rejection Easily	6	5	4	3	2	1
3)	Stand Alone and Account for My Actions	6	5	4	3	2	1
4)	Weigh Options Carefully	6	5	4	3	2	1
5)	Don't Panic-Take Things Slowly	6	5	4	3	2	1
6)	Easy to Talk With About Issues/Problems	6	5	4	3	2	1
7)	Innovative	6	5	4	3	2	1
8)	Promote Team Play	6	5	4	3	2	1
9)	Losing is Very Difficult for Me	6	5	4	3	2	1
10)	Focus on Meeting Objectives	6	5	4	3	2	1
11)	March to the Beat of a Different Drummer	6	5	4	3	2	1
12)	Examine Things Thoroughly	6	5	4	3	2	1
13)	Cool Under Fire-Keep My Composure	6	5	4	3	2	1
14)	Help People When and Where I Can	6	5	4	3	2	1
15)	Creative	6	5	4	3	2	1
16)	Work at Building Team Cohesiveness	6	5	4	3	2	1
17)	Competitive	6	5	4	3	2	1
18)	Move Forward; Don't Give Up	6	5	4	3	2	1
19)	One's Own Person	6	5	4	3	2	1
20)	Put Everything in it's Proper Place	6	5	4	3	2	1
21)	Work Well Under Pressure	6	5	4	3	2	1
22)	Cultivate Friendships Easily	6	5	4	3	2	1
23)	A Person Viewed as Having Good Ideas	6	5	4	3	2	1
24)	Cooperative	6	5	4	3	2	1
25)	Set High Standards for Myself & Others	6	5	4	3	2	1
26)	Take Advantage of Opportunities	6	5	4	3	2	1
27)	Can Stand My Ground	6	5	4	3	2	1
28)	Make Sure of Accuracy	6	5	4	3	2	1
29)	Predictable like Clockwork	6	5	4	3	2	1
30)	People Trust and Come to Me	6	5	4	3	2	1
31)	Possess an Intellectual Curiosity	6	5	4	3	2	1
32)	Collaborative	6	5	4	3	2	1
33)	Always Have Irons in the Fire	6	5	4	3	2	1
34)	Like Finishing What I Start	6	5	4	3	2	1

6. This is <u>Definitely like</u> Me;   5. This is <u>Usually like</u> Me;   4. This is <u>Slightly like</u> Me
3. This is <u>Very Little like</u> Me;   2.This is <u>Not like</u> Me ©   1.This is the <u>Opposite</u> of Me

35)	Have a Mind of My Own	6	5	4	3	2	1
36)	Like to Investigate Situations	6	5	4	3	2	1
37)	Patient	6	5	4	3	2	1
38)	Empathic- Put Myself in Other's Shoes	6	5	4	3	2	1
39)	Like to Brainstorm	6	5	4	3	2	1
40)	Believe in Working Together	6	5	4	3	2	1
41)	High Want to Succeed	6	5	4	3	2	1
42)	High Will to Succeed	6	5	4	3	2	1
43)	Can Fend for Myself	6	5	4	3	2	1
44)	Detailed	6	5	4	3	2	1
45)	Good with Long Term Projects	6	5	4	3	2	1
46)	A Good Listener	6	5	4	3	2	1
47)	Like to Improve Things	6	5	4	3	2	1
48)	Like to Build Agreement in Groups	6	5	4	3	2	1
49)	High Drive and Ambition	6	5	4	3	2	1
50)	Move Quickly to Achieve Tasks	6	5	4	3	2	1
51)	Like an Unstructured Environment	6	5	4	3	2	1
52)	Compliant	6	5	4	3	2	1
53)	In Control of My Emotions	6	5	4	3	2	1
54)	Show Respect to Others	6	5	4	3	2	1
55)	Analyze Situations	6	5	4	3	2	1
56)	Don't Believe in Autocratic Rule	6	5	4	3	2	1
57)	No Grass Grows Under My Feet	6	5	4	3	2	1
58)	Do Everything Possible to Win	6	5	4	3	2	1
59)	Operate as a Self Manager	6	5	4	3	2	1
60)	Practical Minded	6	5	4	3	2	1
61)	Believe that Haste Makes Waste	6	5	4	3	2	1
62)	Good Conversationalist	6	5	4	3	2	1
63)	Learn for Knowledge Sake	6	5	4	3	2	1
64)	Team Focused	6	5	4	3	2	1
65)	Like to Be in Control	6	5	4	3	2	1
66)	Push for Results	6	5	4	3	2	1
67)	Don't Like Supervision	6	5	4	3	2	1
68)	Technically Oriented	6	5	4	3	2	1
69)	Stay with It-Don't Blow Up	6	5	4	3	2	1
70)	Put People at Ease	6	5	4	3	2	1
71)	Can Think Out of the Box	6	5	4	3	2	1
72)	Like People to Engage and Share	6	5	4	3	2	1
73)	Like Authority and to Be in Charge	6	5	4	3	2	1
74)	Energetic Person-Lift Spirit of Others	6	5	4	3	2	1
75)	Strong Will	6	5	4	3	2	1
76)	Careful Not to Make Mistakes	6	5	4	3	2	1
77)	Even Temperament and Steady	6	5	4	3	2	1
78)	Bring Out the Best in Others	6	5	4	3	2	1
79)	Like Mental Challenges	6	5	4	3	2	1
80)	United We Stand, Divided We Fall	6	5	4	3	2	1

The Mulligan Leadership Personality Profile
Calculate Your Scores Below for Each of the Eight Personality Traits

Listed below are *eight personality traits*. There are 10 phrases on the survey for each trait. The related 10 numbers are listed under each of the eight traits below

- ❖ If you marked a 6, place 5 points by the phrase number below
- ❖ If you marked a 5, place 4 points by the phrase number below;
- ❖ If you marked a 4, place 3 points by the phrase number below;
- ❖ If you marked a 3, place 2 points by the phrase number below;
- ❖ If you marked a 2, place 1 points by the phrase number below;
- ❖ If you marked a 1, place 0 points by the phrase number below

Add up all the points to learn your total score for that particular personality trait.

Competitiveness/Aggressiveness (See the Corresponding Numbered Phrases Below)
1_____ 9_____ 17_____ 25_____ 33_____ 41_____ 49_____ 57_____ 65_____ 73_____
Total Points_____

Determined/Persistent (See the Numbered Corresponding Phrases Below)
2._____ 10_____ 18_____ 26_____ 34_____ 42_____ 50_____ 58_____ 66_____ 74_____
Total Points_____

Independent /Self Directed (See the Numbered Corresponding Phrases Below)
3._____ 11_____ 9_____ 27_____ 35_____ 43_____ 51_____ 59_____ 67_____ 75_____
Total Points_____

Detailed/Thorough/Technical (See the Numbered Corresponding Phrases Below)
4_____ 12_____ 20_____ 28_____ 36_____ 44_____ 52_____ 60_____ 68_____ 76_____
Total Points_____

Patient/Self Control (See the Numbered Corresponding Phrases Below)
5_____ 13_____ 21_____ 29_____ 37_____ 45_____ 53_____ 61_____ 69_____ 77_____
Total Points_____

Helper/Service Oriented (See the Numbered Corresponding Phrases Below)
6_____ 14_____ 22_____ 30_____ 38_____ 46_____ 54_____ 62_____ 70_____ 78_____
Total Points_____

Innovative/Creative/Strategic (See the Numbered Corresponding Phrases Below)
7_____ 15_____ 23_____ 31_____ 39_____ 47_____ 55_____ 63_____ 71_____ 79_____
Total Points_____

Team Builder and Player (See the Numbered Corresponding Phrases Below)
8_____ 16_____ 24_____ 32_____ 40_____ 48_____ 56_____ 64_____ 72_____ 80_____
Total Points_____

Your total score for each trait should be 0 (Opposite of Me) to 50.(Definitely Like Me).
Write your total score for each trait on the following page and identify the level where you perceive yourself functioning at this time. You will be placed in Level One to Level Five.

Your Scores and Functioning Level on Eight Personality Traits

We have combined your eighty answers into eight personality traits. Your total points should be placed in the right column below. Based on your total score, you will fall into one of five levels. The higher your total points and level, the more you are like the trait. The lower your total points and level, the less likely you resemble the trait. The score range is 0 to 50. Keep in mind that this profile represents the perceptions you have of yourself and is not a test of right and wrong answers. Ask your parents to fill out the survey and learn if they see you the same way you see yourself.

	50	40	30	20	10	0 Points
Eight Personality Measures	Definitely Like Me	Usually Like Me	Somewhat- Like Me	Very Little Like Me	Not Like or Opposite of Me	
Competitive-Enterprising - A High Want to Achieve and be # 1	Level 5	Level 4	Level 3	Level 2	Level 1	
Determined- A High Will to Achieve and be # 1	Level 5	Level 4	Level 3	Level 2	Level 1	
Independent/ Self-Directed	Level 5	Level 4	Level 3	Level 2	Level 1	
Detailed/Thorough/ Technical	Level 5	Level 4	Level 3	Level 2	Level 1	
Patient/Self Control	Level 5	Level 4	Level 3	Level 2	Level 1	
Helpful/ Service Oriented	Level 5	Level 4	Level 3	Level 2	Level 1	
Innovative/Creative	Level 5	Level 4	Level 3	Level 2	Level 1	
Team Builder/ Player- Collaborative	Level 5	Level 4	Level 3	Level 2	Level 1	
	50	40	30	20	10	0

"TRAITS"

If you fall at level 5 or at Level 4 with a score of 30 and above, your behavior is more like the trait being described. A Level 3 places you in the slightly/somewhat range of likeness. If you fall at Level 1 or 2 with a score of 20 or less, you view yourself as not like or opposite of the trait being described. You need to evaluate the situation you are in at the moment and ask yourself what is the best behavior to display in this role or situation at this time.

Competitive /Assertive Trait©

Competitive/ Assertive-A High Want To Be at the Top

Personality Measure	Definitely Like Me	Usually Like Me	Somewhat Like Me	Very Little Like Me	Not Like Me	Score
Competitive- A high want to succeed.	Level 5	Level 4	Level 3	Level 2	Level 1	

Range	50	40	30	20	10	0

An individual who puts himself/herself at a level 5 or 4 on the *Competitive Scale* is saying that he/she can compete:

- In a competitive and highly stressful situation
- Against others to be accepted in the college of their choice.
- Against others in the class room for the grade and overall G.P.A. he/she desires.
- Against others on campus to be elected or appointed to the leadership positions desired.
- Against others to win over a significant person they want to date
- Against the rigors of college and graduate on the date they set for themselves.
- Against other college graduates and obtain the job desired
- Against others at work and move up the career ladder

Scores at the 5 and 4 indicate you are a *self starter* and have a *high want* to succeed and *be at the top of your class*. You will set the performance bar high for yourself and be able to withstand and handle higher levels of self-imposed pressure and stress to meet your college and work objectives.

You would be described as competitive, enterprising, assertive, tough minded and goal oriented. You might be so goal-oriented that you could appear abrasive at times to others as you strive to achieve your desired results. You will display creative ways to reach your goals and be very critical of your own performance if things don't go as smoothly as you want them to go.

The *competitive trait* is extremely important when operating as a *self manager* and *team unit leader* in college or at work. You will want to set the vision, strategies and growth objectives for yourself as well as the groups you lead. At work, you will want to align the organization and select the people who will execute the growth plan. You will want to establish a performance standard for those who report to you and others in the organization.

The *competitive trait* is also important in being a *team member leader*. Even though team member leaders are not responsible for everyone on the team, they are accountable for what they do as a player on the team. In essence, team members are asked to be competitive and step up to become an expert leader in a special work area so the team unit objectives are met. *Team member leaders* will have the chance to set the performance bar for themselves in an area where they have knowledge, experience and skills. If you are put in the right position, you will become competitive and a leader in your field.

The competitive trait is important if you desire a *competitive sales position*. It reflects how hard you would prospect for or go after business. The reason many people don't go into sales is that don't like prospecting or going after the customers.

An Individual that places himself/herself at a **level 3** on the *competitive scale* is saying "I work best in a well monitored and highly structured work situation. I will be somewhat assertive in setting and meeting standards that I set for myself and those standards imposed on me by the college and company. I will be somewhat self evaluative and critical of myself. While being goal oriented, I would seek traditional channels to achieve my goals. I most likely would be more comfortable in a middle management position than a senior executive position. I am competitive enough to manage and motivate staff to meet a team unit plan.

An individual that places himself/herself at a **level 2 or 1** on the *competitive scale* is saying" I need to be placed in a structured situation where I feel comfortable. Put me in a class or work position, where I have knowledge, skills and talent to compete against others. . I can operate as a self manager and member leader in an environment where I know I can achieve what is asked of me. I see myself more in a supportive team member leadership and service role than a team unit leader ship role.

Recommendations for College Success
Recommendations for those at Level 5 , 4:and 3
1. Establish your priorities and then create goals and a plan of action to achieve your goals. Because of your nature, you might have a tendency to get involved in too many things and this can prevent you from achieving at the performance level you expect from yourself.
2. Because you enjoy doing a lot of things, read about good time management, principles and practice them in your every day activities.
3. Seek leadership positions on campus so you can develop your leadership/management skills.
4. Learn how to be patient with others. Highly competitive people like to move at a faster pace and aggressive people can bully others.
5. While in school, identify and learn to participate in activities that can help you relax and reduce self-imposed stress.
6. You might have what many psychologists call as an "A" type personality. If you establish goals too high and not allow yourself enough time to reach them, you will create unnecessary stress on yourself. Therefore, establish realistic goals and timelines.
7. You should be cognizant of the rules and regulations of the school. If you don't like certain rules, learn how to work within the system to change them.
8. Since you like to take charge, set up study groups and the career advancement networking group to help each other land internships and jobs.

Recommendations for those at Level 2 and 1:
1. You like to agree with and please people. Don't do everything people tell or ask you to do. For example, if your academic advisor says you should take certain courses—ask why—study the curriculum guide and make sure the program is right for you. If you need to study and someone in your room says "let's go get a coke or beer", learn to say "no".
2. Learn how to be assertive and sell you ideas. Take a course in debate or a number of communication courses. Read a lot. Learn how to use facts to back up what you say.
3. Organize yourself (curriculum, extra-curricular activities, social life), establish a daily routine to help you avoid high pressure situations and don't give up easily. Stand your ground.
4. You would probably enjoy support positions in organizations such as Secretary, Treasurer, and Vice President. However, once in a while go for the Presidency.
5. Learn to take on only those responsibilities that you feel comfortable in handling.
At what level did you place yourself on the competitive scale? Can you be competitive enough to meet the challenges of college and graduate with a good job?

DETERMINED/PERSISTENT TRAIT©

Determined/ Persistent – A High Will To Be at the Top

Personality Measure	Definitely Like Me	Usually Like Me	Somewhat Like Me	Very Little Like You	Not Like Me	Score
Determined- A high will to succeed.	Level 5	Level 4	Level 3	Level 2	Level 1	
Range	50	40	30	20	10	0

An individual who puts himself/herself at a level 5 or 4 on the *Determined Scale* is saying that he/she is determined to persist;
- Until he/she is accepted in the college and academic program of choice
- Until he/she meets his/her college objectives
- In the class room until he/she obtains the grade and overall G.P.A. he/she desires.
- Until elected or appointed to the desired leadership positions on campus
- Against the rigors of college and graduate on a targeted date
- To find a good job after college graduation
- To meet the expectations of the boss so it's possible to move up the career ladder.

Scores at the 5 and 4 levels indicate that:
- You have a <u>high will to succeed</u> and be # one.
- You are persistent
- You are determined and hard driving.
- You have a sense of urgency to achieve a task.
- You are eager and active in pursuing the completion of your task.
- You are focused.
- You will raise the energy and the intensity level of those around you.
- You continuously pursue meeting an objective.
- You want to take the organization and people to greater heights.
- Your boss and team mates/colleagues can depend on you to help them reach the objectives.

The *determined/persistent trait* is important in being a *self manager* and *unit leader*. If you are working in the unit leadership/ manager role, you have to start out setting achievable and believable objectives with team members. People must believe the objectives can be met and they will work harder to achieve them.

The *determined/persistent trait* is important in being a *team member*. Any team member can raise the intensity level and performance of the team. If the team unit leader and manager is fairly laid back and does not provide the intensity and energy to raise each team member's level of performance, team members need to step up to push their fellow employees. Michael Jordan of the Chicago Bulls would not allow his team to quit when they got behind in a game. He talked to them, asked them to step it up another notch and willed the team to victory. Each team member must look at how determined, persistent and focused they are when achieving their own objectives as well as the team unit's determination to their objectives. The determination or persistence of team members to win or be the best can overcome the lack of talent on the team.

34

The *determined/persistent trait* is important in being in competitive sales. Once you meet with customers, you have to be persistent in asking for the order. Being persistent is related to being an excellent closer as you try to sell something to a customer or an idea to a colleague during a meeting.

An Individual that places himself/herself at a **level 3** on the *determined scale* is saying "I don't see myself as some one who pushes himself/herself extremely hard to get the job done. I will attempt to accomplish the task but after a while, I might give up. If I was excited or passionate about achieving a particular task or objective, I would work harder to achieve it.

An individual that places himself/herself at a **level 2 or 1** on the *competitive scale* is saying" I don't see myself as a very determined and persistent person. One's perception of being able to do the task or meet the objective will play a part in a person level of persistence and determination.

Recommendations for College Success
Recommendations for those at a Level 5, 4 and 3
1. Select an academic program and major where you are determined to be successful.
2. You might want to join the Honors College so you are challenged.
3. You should be persistent in filling leadership positions on campus so you develop your group leadership and management skills.
4. Place yourself in situations that will develop your academic potential. Select an academic schedule and professors that will challenge and prepare you for graduate or professional school. Individuals who are determined to succeed are more likely to graduate from college and finish a Masters or Ph.D. program.

Recommendations for those at Level 2 and 1.
1. Select an academic program and major where you have a high chance to succeed. If you are really interested in the subject matter and see relevancy in the course work, your will be more determined to do well. This is extremely important to those who might give up to easily.
2. Don't take an academic schedule that is too difficult. If you become discouraged quickly, you might give up and fall behind in your work. This spells disaster. Remember, one success builds on another.
3. You should not give up quickly when you meet obstacles. There is always someone that is willing to help you if you ask for help. We have known lots of people who made bad grades in college their freshman year and continued to obtain a Ph.D. However, they were smart enough to ask for help and grew academically going onto graduate or professional school. Don't give up! Stay the course!

At what level did you place yourself on the determined/persistent scale? Can you be determined or persistent enough to meet the challenges of college, graduate on your target date and find a good job at graduation? Where can you improve on this scale?

INDEPENDENT / SELF DIRECTED TRAIT©

Independent/Self Directed-prefer to manage oneself without supervision

Personality Measure	Definitely Like Me	Usually Like Me	Somewhat Like Me	Very Little Like You	Not Like Me	Score
Independent/ Self-Directed	Level 5	Level 4	Level 3	Level 2	Level 1	

Range   ← 50   ← 40   ← 30   ← 20   ← 10   ← 0

An individual who puts himself/herself at a level 5 or 4 on the *Independent Scale* is saying he/she

- Can find their way to the financial aid office and other important offices on campus
- Can make a list of people on campus that can help them when needed
- Can establish a *to do list* each day and meet all the tasks on the list
- Can organize their room and make sure everything is in a good place to save time
- Can do homework by himself/herself and turn reports in on time
- Can operate as a Self Manager
- Can handle the rigors of college and graduate on the date they set for themselves.
- Can take the steps to land a good job at college graduation.
- Can operate as a Career Manage from college to retirement

Scores at the 5 and 4 levels indicate that:
- You like to work alone without supervision.
- You want authority and a wide range of freedom to develop and achieve your plan.
- You would want the freedom from your parents or boss to run your own show.
- You would like to be in charge of your own destiny.
- You are strong minded and firm in the way you do things.
- You are independent and self directed
- You would have problems with an autocratic leader or domineering boss.
- You want to develop your own procedures and methods of doing things.
- You like planning, organizing and establishing your own day to day structure.
- You might have difficulty operating as a team player and being cooperative
- You would need to set up a Partnership Expectation PAC with your advisor, parents and boss
- You would view yourself as a self- starter and self manager.
- You would enjoy managing self managers and operating as a macro-manager and not a micro-manage where you need to do a lot of coaching. This means you would like being a senior executive more than a manager.
- You could operate on your own to sell products/services or on a special project.

The *self directed/independent trait is key to being a self manager and important in both leadership roles.* If you are working in the unit leadership/manager role, you want each team member to become a *self manager and expert leader* in his particular field so you can turn them loose without constantly supervising them. You can then spend more time monitoring the progress of the unit and communicating with others in the company and customers.

36

The *team member leader* needs to work on mastering his/her assigned tasks and meeting the objectives he/she and the advisor/boss set when the year first started. The team member needs to work on becoming a self manager so the advisor/boss can empower and provides complete authority to the person. One-On-One meetings between the unit leader/manager and team member can help the team member move to an expert leadership status and operating alone.

The *self directed/independent scale* is another personality trait important in being successful in *sales*. Sales people are usually assigned to special territory and they have to learn to operate on their own without any supervision. People who are independent love operating in their own territory being accountable for their results and reporting to the boss when it necessary.

An individual that places himself/herself at a **level 3** on the *independent scale* is saying "I don't need a lot of supervision but I do need to know what my advisor and boss expects from me. I do operate better in a team oriented environment where there is a lot of communication".

An individual that places himself/herself at a **level 2 or 1** on the *independent scale* is saying" I like to work closely with my advisor/boss and others on the team.. I thrive better in a structured situation where the rules and policies are clearly laid out and I know exactly what my advisor/boss expects from me".

Recommendations for College Success
Recommendations for those at a Level 5, 4 and 3
1. Learn the rules and policies of the college and abide by them.
2. Investigate the courses that offer an independent study.
3. Don't be so strong minded and independent that you will not accept help when you need it.
4. Learn how to adapt, get along and listen to people in power positions.
5. Seek out leadership positions on campus and learn how to build team cohesiveness and team play in the organizations you lead.
6. Learn how to be a follower as well as a leader.

Recommendations for those at Level 2 and 1.
1. When the opportunity exists, try your hand at being a unit leader as well as a follower.
2. Take a risk once in awhile and do more activities on your own rather depending on others for advice and support.
3. Learn to operate as a self manager.
4. Learn to operate as a career manager.
5. Learn to operate as a finder on campus so you don't need to depend on others to tell you what to do.
6. Develop a Partnership Expectation PAC with your parents and advisor and spell out what you will do for yourself versus what Mom and Dad will do for you.

At what level did you place yourself on independent scale? Can you be self directed enough to meet the challenges of college, graduate from college on your target date, find a good job at graduation and do work assignments by yourself? Where can you improve?

DETAILED/THOROUGH/TECHNICAL TRAIT©

Detailed/Thorough/Technical-Nothing Gets Past Me/Very Practical

Personality Measure	Definitely Like Me	Usually Like Me	Somewhat Like Me	Very Little Like Me	Not Like Me	Score
Detailed/ Through/ Technical	Level 5	Level 4	Level 3	Level 2	Level 1	

Range   50   40   30   20   10   0

An individual who puts himself/herself at a level 5 or 4 on the *Detailed Scale* is saying he/she

- Can investigate and make a list of people on campus that can help when the situation calls for it
- Can set a detailed *to do list* each day and meet all the tasks on the list
- Can organize room, do homework and turn reports in on time
- Can develop a networking list freshmen year and add to the list every year
- Can monitor and take the courses needed to graduate on the graduation target date
- Can explore career fields and majors in technology, business detail, science and the security area.
- Can take the steps to land a good job at college graduation.
- Can operate as a Career Manager from college to retirement

Scores at the 5 and 4 levels indicate that:
- Your orientation would be toward detail, technical, factual, analytical and investigative work.
- You would enjoy solving intellectual challenges by investigating the facts and concepts associated with a problem or situation.
- You would weigh your options carefully when making decisions.
- You would make sure of accuracy.
- You would use your technical orientation to good use.
- You would set up policies and procedures so people know how to operate in the organization.
- You would enjoy doing research and gathering data to help the organization make decisions.
- You would make sure the organization was compliant with government and banking regulations
- You would work hard to keep the unit/organization under budget and profitable.
- Your boss would have confidence in assigning you tasks and listening to what you say.
- You would operate as a tactical strategist which requires day to day plans to get results.

The *detailed/thorough/technical trait* is important in being a self manager and group leader. If you are working in the unit leadership/manager role, you want to make sure you have done your homework when you hire people, set objectives and strategies and move forward to execute your plan. Unit/manager leaders need to understand new technology and be more into detail knowing the processes, procedures and policies set by the organization. This includes knowing the process and procedure to follow when recruiting, developing, promoting or releasing someone. Organizations can spend more money than they need to spend each year on litigation because unit leaders didn't follow the rules set by their organization.

Group leaders also need to be more thorough when they purchase another company to expand market share. Many organizations have been hurt financially or gone out of business because they paid too much money on an acquisition. Unit leaders also need to be effective as a time manager.

Team members leaders need to be detailed and thorough in mastering their assigned tasks so the organization can be successful. Organizations depend on team member leaders to handle much of the detail and investigative work so the team unit leaders can develop realistic plans and long term strategies.

The *detail* personality trait is also important in being a *sales person*. You have to keep track of your orders and customers and manage your time and appointments.

Recommendations for College Success
Recommendations for those at a Level 5, 4 and 3
1. You might enjoy a curriculum in business detail (actuary, accounting, economics, finance etc.), computer science, engineering, the health fields, investigative work, underwriting and other technical fields which require people to be more thorough in what they do.
2. Since you like detail, take notes in class and establish good study habits.
3. Take some internships in positions that require detail and investigative work.
4. Use you research skills to learn about yourself and the world of work
5. Put yourself in leadership positions on campus that requires detail work

Recommendations for those at Level 2 and 1.
1. Since you might not like detail, force yourself to take good notes in class, establish a time to study each day and organize the area where you study.
2. You would probably like courses that are not math, science and technically oriented.
3. If you have trouble with courses that are detail in nature, don't hesitate to attend the class twice in the same day if your schedule permits.
4. You will make a lot of decisions in your life time. You should keep in mind that you should gather as much information or data you can before you make a decision. You don't want to make decisions from the seat of your pants.
5. If you are not detail oriented, work on being more organized in college. It will carry over to work later.
6. Learn how to conduct an informational and exploratory interview to learn about occupations, career fields and positions. The research will help you make better career decisions.

At what level did you place yourself on the detailed/thorough scale? Can you be organized enough to meet the challenges of college, graduate from college on your target date and find a good job at graduation and be thorough in your job at work? Where can you improve?

PATIENT/SELF CONTROL ©

PATIENT/SELF CONTROL-NEVER LOSE MY COOL

Personality Measure	Definitely Like Me	Usually Like Me	Somewhat Like Me	Very Little Like Me	Not Like Me	Score
Patient/Self Control	Level 5	Level 4	Level 3	Level 2	Level 1	

Range   50   40   30   20   10   0

An individual who puts himself/herself at a level 5 or 4 on the *Patient Scale* is saying he/she

- Has the patience to complete an assignment that takes a long time to do
- Has the patience to make a *to do list* each day and meet all the tasks on the list
- Has the patience to organize his/her room and make sure everything is in a good place
- Has the patience to finish and do a good job on his/her homework without being interrupted
- Has the patience to sit and listen to a friend and help them solve an issue or problem
- Has the patience to control his/her emotions during a heated discussion.
- Has the patience to make important decisions in a logical state and not in an emotional one

Scores at the 5 and 4 levels indicate that:

- You don't panic, reflect a calm, steady, unhurried, relaxed, stable and patient manner.
- You can tolerate tasks that require longer periods of time to complete.
- You would take the time to learn about a person and thus be an effective helper or manager.
- You would listen to people for longer periods of time helping them explore and understand their situation before developing appropriate action steps.
- You would be viewed as approachable when one needs to talk about a problem.
- You would enjoy coaching employees and building champion performers.
- You keep your composure during intense discussions and not make hasty decisions.
- You would take things slowly and would not push the panic button.
- You would be mentally disciplined.
- You would be patient with class mates, customers and fellow workers.

The *Patient/Self Control trait* is important as a self manager and group leader. If you are working in the unit leadership/ manager's role, you want to make sure you are patient and in self control at all times. When executives become angry and frustrated, they can make decisions that can come back to haunt them. There have been stories about CEOs throwing pencils and swearing at their senior management staff as well as firing them on the spot because the sales numbers were not good. Unit leaders/managers need to work on their One on One Management skills and take the time to help direct reports /team members become expert leaders in their field. This takes *patience* and being in *self control*. How many good decisions have you made when you were mad or angry? We would guess not very many.

Team member leaders need to be patient and in self control when their bosses, colleagues and customers say stupid things to them. In an article in USA Today 2011, 80 % of the workers said they participate in an uncivil like work environment. Team members need to be patient and in self control when working directly with people that are not civil. Employees who can control their emotions with customers and fellow employees are a real asset to an organization.

The *patience/self control* trait is equally as important when working in sales. You have to make a lot of sales calls and your potential customers receive a lot of calls each day. They can treat you very rudely. When you keep your composure and treat these individuals with dignity and respect, you will have a better chance of getting in for an interview.

Recommendations for College Success
Recommendations for those at a Level 5, 4 and 3
1. You might enjoy a curriculum in human resources, police work, counseling, social work, teaching, business management, banking, retail work, the ministry, student personnel work in higher education, high school counseling and consulting work since you have rated yourself high in patience. These areas do a lot of listening to people and helping them solve their problems.
2. Other jobs that require a lot of patience is business detail, computer work, engineering, research, the health fields and being an undertaker. What other jobs require patience?
3. You should display your patience with fellow students when they are expressing themselves. If you show that you care about what they say, you will develop an engaging relationship with them. Being able to engage with people is an important asset in the world of work today.
4. You should practice your patience with fellow students when your group is trying to make a decision about something. You will be more respected and all the information given can help the group make a wiser decision.
3. The more you develop your patience with people, the better group leader and counselor/coach you will become in the future.
4. Being a patient person, you should take the time to develop a strategic graduation plan
5. Being a patient person, you should develop a step by step plan to be employed at graduation.

Recommendations for those at Level 2 and 1.
1. If you are not a patient person, this is a feature of yourself you should really work on improving. More people are fired because they lack self control at work.
2. If you are not a patient person, you need to place yourself in career positions that call for quick responses like sales, stock brokerage work, coaching and managing organizations.
3. If you are not a patient person, you can find yourself being critical of professors, administrators and friends very quickly. Give people some slack.
4. You will make a lot of decisions in your life time. You should keep in mind that you need to be patient and gather as much information or data you can before you make a decision. You don't want to make a decision that will haunt you the rest of your life.

At what level did you place yourself on the patient scale? Can you be patient enough to listen to others, meet the challenges of college, graduate from college on your target date and find a good job at graduation? Where can you improve?

HELPER/PERFORMANCE FACILITATOR TRAIT©

Helper/Performance Facilitator-Bringing Out the Best in Those Around You

Personality Measure	Definitely Like Me	Usually Like Me	Somewhat Like Me	Very Little Like Me	Not Like Me	Score
Performance Facilitator and Helper	Level 5	Level 4	Level 3	Level 2	Level 1	

Range	50	40	30	20	10	0

An individual who puts himself/herself at a level 5 or 4 on the *Helper Scale* is saying he/she

- Looks for ways to create a common bond with others
- Is perceived as someone who cares about people
- Is perceived as a trustworthy and authentic person
- Is perceived as objective and not bias when someone is talking to them
- Knows that you can harm as well as help someone with what you say or don't say
- Doesn't tell people what to do but helps them come up with a plan to solve their own issue
- Functions on helping individuals increase understanding of their situation so they can develop the most appropriate plan to solve their issue or problem

Scores at the 5 and 4 levels indicate that:

- You would be someone a person would seek out to discuss and solve a problem or issue.
- You would be perceived as a person who is a good sounding board.
- You would help someone explore, understand and solve their situation without giving premature advice that could be harmful.
- You would have the capability to respond with empathy to a person who is in an unpleasant emotional state and move them to a logical state so they can think clearly.
- You would help people establish, execute and meet growth objectives.
- You would be described as supportive and accepting of others.
- You would enjoy being in a position to take care of the behind the scenes work and keep the team on course to meet the objectives.
- You would enjoy managing and coaching people so they become a champion performer.
- You would like servicing customers and helping fellow colleagues in the organization.
- You would want to build a helping and performance facilitating work environment.
- You would spot talent in people and help them develop it.
- You would help people move toward their ultimate career position.
- You would build systems to identify talented people and grow them so the organization stays competitive and successful in the years ahead.
- You would confront someone if they are not walking their talk.
- You would challenge individuals to become the best they can be.

The *Helper/Performance Facilitator trait* is important in being a self manager and group leader. Everyone in an organization should go through a helping and performance facilitation training program. It is important for employees to learn how to build working relationships with each other, be able to focus listen and target respond when colleagues are talking in a one- on- one session or team meeting so in-depth understanding occurs and wise plans can be developed. If there are good working relationships built and employees help each other execute a well conceived plan, the team unit/organization will have a better chance of being successful. At what level did you place yourself on the helper/performance facilitator scale above? At what level do you need to operate effectively in your present and future position?

Recommendations for College Success
Recommendations for those at a Level 5, 4 and 3
1. You might enjoy a curriculum in government, servant of the community, human resources, counseling, social work, teaching, business management, banking, retail work, the ministry, student personnel work in higher education, high school counseling and consulting work since you have rated yourself high on the helper/performance facilitator scale. People in these roles do a lot of listening to people and helping them solve their problems and issues.
2. Establish support groups and emphasize the importance of operating as a performance facilitator or helping communicator with one another.
3. You should display your attending skills with fellow students when they are expressing themselves. If you show that you care about what they say, you will develop an engaging relationship with them. Being able to engage with people is an important asset in the world of work today.
4. You should practice your listening and responding skills with fellow students when an individual or group is trying to make a decision about something. You will help the individual or group make a wiser decision.
3. The more you develop your listening and responding skills with people, the better group leader and counselor/coach you will become in the future.
4. Being a helpful person, help yourself and others graduate from college.
5. Being a helpful person, help yourself and others be employed at graduation.

Recommendations for those at Level 2 and 1.
1. If you are not a helpful person and performance facilitator, this is a feature of yourself you should really work on improving. More people are fired because they lack human relations skills.
2. If you are not a performance facilitator or helping communicator, you can purchase Dr. Mulligan's book *Sharpening My One-On-One Performance Facilitation and Helping Communication Skills*. He has assessments in the book plus a *Model* you can read about and execute.
3. People make a lot of decisions in their life time and if you can sharpen your performance facilitation and helping communication skills, you can help a lot of people make good decisions.

At what level did you place yourself on the helper/performance facilitation scale? Are you operating at a harmful or helpful level when helping others make good decisions, solve problems, make plans and succeed? Where can you improve?

INNOVATIVE/CREATIVE/STRATEGIC TRAIT©

Innovative/Creative- An idea person who improves processes, products and service.

Personality Measure	Definitely Like You	Usually Like You	Somewhat Like You	A Little Like You	Not Like You	Score
Innovative/ Creative/ Strategic	Level 5	Level 4	Level 3	Level 2	Level 1	

Range	50	40	30	20	10	0

An individual who puts himself/herself at a level 5 or 4 on the *Innovative Scale* is saying he/she

- Likes to be creative
- Values imagination and innovation
- Likes to make improvements on what is presently being done
- Can see the big picture and believes strategic thinking is critical to any organization
- Likes to brainstorm ideas and problems and come up with the best solutions

Scores at the 5 and 4 levels indicate that:

- You would operate as a visionary and strategic thinker, one who is always studying the landscape, sees the big picture and helps the organization become what it should become and be.
- You would like to brainstorm and come up with ideas that can help the unit/organization.
- You would be looking to improve processes in the organization
- You would be a critical thinker, one who can digest, analyze and synthesize information and use the findings to make future plans..
- You would help people and your organization improve the way things are done.
- You would push people to think out of the box and be more innovative.
- You would like have the opportunity to be creative and work with ideas in your daily work.
- You would think things out before taking action.
- You would be curious about how things work.
- You would keep your antenna up to anticipate and make changes that are necessary..

The *Innovative/Creative/Strategic trait* is important in both leadership roles. If you are working in the unit leadership/manager's role, you want to make sure you work with others to create a vision of what the unit/organization should be like in the future and develop a plan to get there. The competition will continue to think of ways to be the best in the industry so your organization needs to tap it's brain power as well. Unit leadership needs to find the best minds and bring out the thinking of the present employees. Unit leaders also need to continue to think of how each department and the total organization can get better and stay ahead of the competition. Employees hear about continuous improvement but it needs to be practiced. Many employees have great ideas but no one solicits them.

When team unit leaders sit down to manage their direct reports one-on- one, this is the time to ask each person how they can improve what they are doing and how the unit and organization can be improved. Psychologists say people use about 15% of their potential. This is because many unit leaders look at their employees as grinders rather than asking them how they and the unit/organization can do things faster and better. There is an old saying "there is no one as smart as all of us". Unit leaders need to meet with direct reports and conduct "think tanks" to pull new and creative ideas out of them. Many team members need to also become tactical strategists creating practical step by step plans to help the organization.

44

Recommendations for College Success

Recommendations for those at a Level 5, 4 and 3

1. You might enjoy a curriculum in management, advertising and marketing, promotional work, packaging, engineering, psychology, investigative/security work, banking, retail work, the ministry, web design and in positions that require working with ideas and innovation.
2. You might put yourself in positions on campus that require innovation and thinking out of the box. This could be serving on a number of student committees.
3. You should form special groups on campus such as study groups, and a group that helps one another find internships and good jobs at and after graduation.
4. You should also place yourself in marketing and promotion positions because you would enjoy creating and executing marketing campaigns where you are advertising events or people.
5. Look for internship positions where you can use your creative and innovative skills
6. Work with administrators on campus to raise money and promote the college
7. Join the entrepreneur program on campus so you can put your creative skills to the test.
8. Develop a strategy where you can graduate on your time line with little debt.

Recommendations for those at Level 2 and 1.

1. If you are not a innovative person, you can help people with ideas see the practical side of their plan or idea.
2. You can keep your knowledge up to date on certain areas so you can add important information to the conversation when individuals or groups are making important decisions.
3. Try to be open to new ideas and make them better.
4. Work on positive reinforcement for people who have really good ideas.
5. Work on becoming more creative and innovative.

At what level did you place yourself on the innovative scale? Can you be innovative enough to meet the challenges of college, graduate from college on your target date and find a good job at graduation? Where can you improve?

TEAM PLAYER/COLLABORATIVE©

TEAM BUILDER AND TEAM PLAYER- THERE IS NO ONE SMARTER THAN ALL OF US

Personality Measure	Definitely Like You	Usually Like You	Somewhat Like You	A Little Like You	Not Like You	Score
Team Builder/ Player	Level 5	Level 4	Level 3	Level 2	Level 1	

Range ← **50** ← **40** ← **30** ← **20** ← **310** ← **0**

An individual who puts himself/herself at a level 5 or 4 on the *Team Player Scale* is saying he/she

- Looks for ways to bring people together
- Is perceived as someone who is collaborative
- Likes team cohesiveness and team play
- Wants everyone on the team to be successful
- Believes everyone on the team has a role to play and if everyone does their job, all benefit

Scores at the 5 and 4 levels indicate that:

- You would promote the sharing of ideas
- You would concentrate on building team cohesiveness
- You would reinforce continuous team play.
- You would create a collaborative and democratic work environment.
- You would want everyone on the planning team and being accountable for the results.
- You would encourage acceptance of differences of opinion and divergent thinking.
- You would promote acceptance of cultural and individual differences.
- You would increase emotional involvement in team objective achievement.
- You would put the spot light on the team and would wave the team flag.
- You would enjoy a close working relationship with your boss and team mates.
- You would want to review your job tasks with your boss and be sure of what he/she expects..

The *Team Player/Collaborative trait* is important in both leadership roles. If you are working in the unit leadership/manager's role, you want to make sure you communicate to your direct reports that it is people who play on championship teams that normally get ahead in the world. You can discuss the 1985 Chicago Bears team who won a super bowl. They not only won rings but obtained great jobs after their football days were over and still have good jobs today.

People on team units need to know that if they play together, they and their unit/organization can become the best at what they do. If this happens, their company will want to keep them and other companies will want to recruit them. Senior management likes to keep people who are talented and best in their field.

Another important point is that if you can build a strong working relationship with all the people that work in your unit and help each other and the unit be successful, there will be one person in the group whose career will take off. As that person moves up the management ladder, they will mostly likely take you with them. Your career can rise on the shirt tail of a fellow worker.

The Triangle Team Leadership Model: Becoming Leaders in Our Field is a leadership and performance management system that can transform team members into expert leaders in their fields.

Recommendations for College Success

Recommendations for those at a Level 5, 4 and 3

1. You might enjoy a curriculum in music, physical education/coaching, management, human resources, counseling psychology, social work, teaching, banking, retail work, the ministry and consulting work. These areas do a lot of team building.

2. You would like to transform groups into teams.

3. You should do some reading on group dynamics and find assessment instruments that can help you obtain information on individuals in your group so you can understand how the group will work together..

4. You should try to build team cohesiveness and team play on your floor in the residence hall and in any organization you join.

5. You like to be cooperative and this practice will help you in college and the world of work.

6. You should build a group of similar majors to help each other obtain internships and jobs after graduation. Support groups can be very important in career transitioning.

Recommendations for those at Level 2 and 1.

1. If you consider yourself to be a lone wolf, work on being a team member.

2. No one makes it in this world without someone else helping them. Build and develop a network of people who can help you throughout your career journey.

3. Being collaborative is important today in working with people and keeping your job.. Start learning how to be more collaborative starting today.

4. Learn how to put the spotlight on others and you will find more people putting the spotlight on you.

At what level did you place yourself on the team player/ building scale? Can you work with others enough to meet the challenges of college, graduate from college on your target date and find and keep a good job? Where can you improve?

Task Three-

Fill Out the *Personal and Social Maturity Survey*, Self Score It
and Identify Where You Need to Make Changes to Succeed

The Personal and Social Maturity Survey

Please rate yourself on the following 30 statements.   Scale 0 to 6

6.-Definitely Like Me   5.- Usually Like Me   4.- Slightly Like Me

3.-Very Little Like Me   2.- Not Like Me   1.- Definitely Not Like Me

___ 1. I am aware of my interests, skills, experiences, talent, values, and leadership ability.

— 2. I never let things or others upset me so much that I blow up or lose my cool around people.

— 3. I am aware of what motivates me and de-motivates me.

— 4. I am very effective at identifying the feelings of others and stating the feeling words back to them showing empathy.

— 5. I am a good listener and respond accurately to people's messages so they understand their situation more in-depth and can then make better decisions and plans.

— 6. I am aware of my limitations and know what I need to work on to improve myself.

— 7. I am aware of my obsessions and know when I become overly compulsive.

— 8. I am always striving to improve and live up to my potential.

— 9. I am a caring person as I am very sensitive to other people's feelings and thoughts.

— 10. I can negotiate and resolve disagreements.

— 11. I am aware of my emotions and know what places me in different emotional states.

— 12. I can establish my own objectives, plan of action and work structure.

— 13. I am committed to pursuing the growth goals and achieving the objectives set by my team unit and organization.

— 14. I can help others identify their developmental needs and bolster their confidence to be the best they can be.

— 15. I have the ability to inspire and lead individuals and groups.

48

The Personal and Social Maturity Survey Continued

6.-Definitely Like Me   5.- Usually Like Me   4.- Slightly Like Me

3.-Very Little Like Me   2.- Not Like Me   1.- Definitely Not Like Me

___16   I have a strong sense of self worth and know I am capable of being a leader in my class or field..

— 17.   I am accountable for my actions on tasks that need to be completed.

— 18.   I am always ready and alert to act on opportunities that make me, my team and organization better.

— 19.   I can anticipate, recognize and meet the needs of others.

__ 20.   I have the ability to initiate and manage change.

— 21.   I know when I say something that offends others.

— 22.   I am very flexible and adaptable.

— 23.   I am always optimistic and look at the glass as half full instead of half empty.

— 24.   I realize that you can cultivate opportunities and success through people who have different experiences, backgrounds and come from different cultures.

— 25.   I am extremely effective at creating group synergy and pursuing collective goals.

— 26.   I know what career field and positions would be best for me now.

— 27.   I am comfortable with new ideas, approaches and information.

— 28.   I have a high want and high will to win.

— 29.   I am politically astute, being able to read the group's emotional currents and power relationships.

— 30.   I am extremely effective at texting, e-mailing, phoning and staying in touch with friends, family and people who are important to my success at this time.

Please place your answers on the following pages to determine your *Personal and Social Maturity Scores* and Total Score. Rank categories below based on scores.

1.

2.

3.

4.

5.

Determining Your Personal and Social Maturity Scores

Three categories in this assessment make up your **Personal Maturity** and the other *two* involve your **Social Maturity.** Your total score represents your *Personal and Social Maturity* Level. The term *Emotional Intelligence* is similar to *Personal and Social Maturity* and was created by Dr. Daniel Goleman[7]. He defines Emotional Intelligence as "managing feelings so that they are expressed appropriately and effectively, enabling people to work together to accomplish their common goals."

Review Your 30 Answers, Write the Number Answers Below and Calculate Scores for Your Personal and Social Maturity.

<u>**(Determining Your Personal Maturity Score)**</u>
(Three categories)
1.   **Self Awareness**
   - Emotional awareness
   - Accurate self assessment
   - Self confidence

1. _____   6. _____   11. _____   16. _____   21. _____   26. _____
Total Score: _____(write your scores down for the six survey items above and add them up. Your total score will range from 0 to 36)

2.   **Self Regulation**
   - Self control
   - Trustworthiness
   - Conscientiousness
   - Adaptability
   - Innovation

2. _____   7. _____   12. _____   17. _____   22. _____   27. _____
Total Score: _____(write your scores down for the six survey items above and add them up. Your total score will range be from 0 to 36.)

3.   **Motivation**
   - Achievement driven
   - Committed
   - Initiative
   - Optimistic

3. _____   8. _____   13. _____   18. _____   23. _____   28. _____
Total Score: _____ (write your scores down for each of the six survey items above and add them up. Your score will range be from 0 to 36)

<u>(Determining Your Social Maturity Score)</u>

(Two categories)

1.   **Empathy**
   - Understanding other people's feelings
   - Interacting with others
   - Service orientation
   - Leveraging diversity
   - Political awareness

4. _____ 9. _____ 14. _____ 19. _____ 24. _____ 29. _____

Total Score: _____ (write your scores down for each of the six survey items and add them up. Your score will range from 0 to 36.)

2.   **Social Skills**
   - Influence
   - Communication
   - Conflict management
   - Leadership
   - Change catalyst
   - Building bonds
   - Collaboration and cooperation
   - Team building capabilities

4. _____ 10. _____ 15. _____ 20. _____ 25. _____ 30. _____

Total Score: _____ (write your scores down for each of the six survey items above and add them up. Your total score will range from 0 to 36.)

Total Score on the Five Categories

Self Awareness   _____
Self Regulation   _____
Motivation   _____
Empathy   _____
Social Skills   _____
TOTAL SCORE   _____

<u>**Total Personal & Social Maturity Score**</u>

180-150   Extremely mature
149-120   Above average maturity
119-90   Average maturity
89-60   Below average in maturity
59-   Extremely immature

Goleman's Research on Emotional Intelligence
(E.Q. *similar to personal and social maturity*)

Daniel Goleman, in his book: *Working with Emotional Intelligence,* discussed three areas that make us successful on the job. They are:

- I.Q. – our ability to comprehend and learn things quickly
- Technical expertise and experience
- Emotional intelligence

Goleman discovered that emotional intelligence had to do more with emerging as a leader and becoming a star performer than I.Q. and technical expertise.

David McClelland found that outstanding performers were not just strong in initiative or influence but had strengths across the board, which included the five emotional intelligence areas: self-awareness, self-regulation, motivation, empathy and social skills.

McClelland discovered that the emotional competencies that most often led to star status were:

- Initiative, achievement, drive and adaptability
- Influence, team leadership and political awareness
- Empathy, self-confidence and developing others

The two most common traits that prevented people from becoming star performers were:
- Rigidity: These individuals were unable to adapt their style to changes in the organizational culture or to be flexible or to respond to feedback about traits they needed to change or improve. They couldn't listen or learn.

- Poor Relationships: This was the most single frequently mentioned factor. Individuals were being too harshly critical, insensitive or demanding and this alienated those that work for and with that person.

Daniel Goleman conducted research using his competence model with 181 different job positions in 121 companies worldwide. The model asked management to profile excellence for each job. Emotional competence mattered twice as much as I.Q. and expertise. Since 1918, the average I.Q. score in the United States has risen 24 points. Goleman says that as students have grown smarter in I.Q., their emotional intelligence has declined. This means students are growing more lonely, depressed, angry, unruly, nervous, impulsive, aggressive and prone to worry. If this is not corrected, students will be coming to the workplace with lower emotional intelligence (personal and social maturity) which creates a major challenge for companies in the future.

Task four
Analyze What Your Parents Do for You and Develop a Partnership Expectation PAC with Them to Become a Self Manager

What will your parents do for you that you can not do for yourself?
- Will your parents do most of the talking to administrators on campus?
  _____yes _____no
- Will your parents decorate and redecorate your room at college?
  _____yes _____no
- Will your parents call or text you more than once a day to check on you?
  _____yes _____no
- Will your parents talk to your academic advisor more than you?
  _____yes _____no
- Will your parents talk to your professors more than you?
  _____yes _____no
- Will your parents talk on your behalf to your coach or someone in power if you are dissatisfied with something?
  _____yes _____no
- Will your parents help you with your homework at college?
  _____yes _____no
- Will your parents tell you what to do more than you like?
  _____yes _____no

If you answered **no** six out of eight times, you pass with a 75%.

Filling out a Partnership Expectation PAC with Your Parents

Your family is investing a lot of money in your college education. It is a partnership. Your family should sit down together and fill out a *Partnership Expectation Pac* for each year you are in college. This can be part of your *Plan*. You need to know what you can expect from your parents and they need to know what they can expect from you.

<u>**Partnership Expectation PAC – Parent's Pledge**</u> **(make a copy for each year of college)** ©

You can expect the following from your parents:

Financial assistance:
1. _____
2. _____
3. _____

Emotional support to you
1. _____
2. _____
3. _____
4. _____

Doing things for you that need to be done:

    1. _____
    2. _____
    3. _____
    4. _____

Communicating with you:

    1.How often _____
    2.How you communicate _____
    3.What you share with each other _____

Partnership Expectation PAC- Your Pledge ©

My parents can expect the following from me:

Grades for each semester:

    1. _____ Fall Semester
    2. _____ Spring Semester
    3. _____Summer Semester

Financial contribution toward college:

    1. _____Work
    2. _____Scholarships/Grants
    3. _____Loans

Communication with parents:

    1. How often _____
    2. How we communicate _____
    3. What we share with each other _____

Boundaries:

    1. _____
    2. _____
    3. _____

How I spend my time at college:

    1. _____
    2. _____
    3. _____
    4. _____
    5. _____

Coming home:

    1. How often _____
    2. When _____

Release: I will give the college permission to share information about me with my parents.
____yes ____no

I expect to graduate in the year_____ with an overall GPA of_____

Task Five-
Anticipate the Changes Facing You in College, Work and Life and Operate as a Self Manager and Leader

Facing Change

One of the biggest challenges you will face in college, work and life is learning how to anticipate and manage change. The pace of change is so fast today that if you don't have your antenna up to see change coming it will be harder to plan and react to it. Listed below are some changes you will be facing in college, work and life and being a self manager is a way of handling all these changes.

College

You will face many changes when moving through college and graduate school. Some of these changes will include:

- Having over 30 plus professors in undergraduate college and 20 or more professors in graduate school. Each professor will have a different personality, teaching style and criteria for grading.
- Stronger competition in the class room; there is always someone smarter than you. You will continuously compete against smart people.
- Continually meeting new people from different backgrounds and locations; you need to work on your social and interpersonal skills in order to develop a network of friends.
- Helping finance your college education – You need to investigate all the ways you can pay for your higher education and take advantage of them.
- Technological changes – the way people communicate and the many ways classes are now being taught.

Work

You will face many changes when moving through your career journey. Some changes will include:

- Having as many as 30 plus bosses. It is possible you will have a new boss every year. Each boss will have his or her own personality, leadership and management style, and ways of relating to his or her direct reports.
- Two or more career changes; most people today as we have already said will have two or more career changes.
- Working for 6-12 different companies; organizations today buy, sell or merge as part of the business plan.
- Spouses living away from each other because the new assignment means moving to a new location; executives are commuting more and more by plane from work to the family's residence.
- Being out of work at least three or four times in your career journey; companies and organizations are releasing people every day to save costs.

Life

You will face many changes moving through life. Some of these changes will include:

- Your physical appearance; genetics will play a very important part in how you age, but you can play an even more important role in how you look (i.e., exercise, moderate drinking, no smoking, personal hygiene).
- Your educational development; graduating from post-secondary schools to help you meet your career objectives.
- Your financial situation changing from year-to-year; some people might make a modest salary and then be promoted to the senior level making lots of money, only to lose most of it in the stock market. Put money away when you can.
- Organization, family and societal values; as we age, we might see the values of our company, family and society go in different directions.
- What your life will look like after you and/or your spouse retire; agreeing and compromising where you might live, how you spend your finances, and how you spend your time together.

People find it difficult to change because they fear the uncertainty of change and see it as a threat to their security. You as an individual will face change. You can be part of the problem or part of the answer. The choice is yours. The following are some suggestions for meeting the challenge of change.

Why fight it?

Change is a fact of life so learn to live with it. The changes we face in school, work and life will always be a part of our lives so why fight these changes. The way we do things in society, the people around us and the way we do work in our company is going to change; so why fight it? Why not accept change and learn to enjoy change as part of the adventures of life.

See the Bigger Picture

Learn to look at the bigger picture. You'll be a happier individual if you train yourself to hold in your mind the ultimate benefit of change, rather than the fears and hardships that change might temporarily impose.

Develop habits of change.

You live your life by habit. You've trained yourself from infancy to respond and behave as you do. Breaking habits can be unpleasant, so make change a habit. Why not make your life a little more fun by learning to live with change instead of routine?

Look for the benefits in change.

Out of every change comes some benefit to you if you look for it with enough faith and persistence. Look for the bigger and better opportunity rather than becoming mired in self-pity. If you look hard enough at the bright side, positive things will come your way.

Create a Plan to Improve Yourself as a Self Manager/Leader

Please list **three priorities** you need to work on to improve yourself as a self manager/leader

Priority #1:

_____

_____

Please list three action steps you need to take to meet this priority.

1._____

2._____

3._____

Priority #2:

_____

_____

Please list three action steps you need to take to meet this priority.

1._____

2._____

3._____

Priority #3:

_____

_____

Please list three action steps you need to take to meet this priority.

1._____

2._____

3._____

<u>**Goal # Three**</u>-
**Assess and Analyze Yourself as a Career Manager and Identify
Where You Need to Grow to be a Competent Career Manager**

<u>**Page**</u>

59   <u>**Task One**</u>- Fill out the *Career Management Competency Survey* and
          Analyze Your Results and Identify Where You Need Coaching

72   <u>**Task Two**</u>- Learn the *Route 56 Career Management Model* Which
          Can Help You Manage Your Career from College to Retirement

77   <u>**Task Three**</u>-Review the *15 Proven Career Strategies* and Execute These
          Strategies as You Manage Your Career Journey

83   <u>**Task Four**</u>- Develop, Execute and Meet a Growth Plan to Become a
          Career Manager

Task One-
Fill out the *Career PlanningAssessment* and
Analyze Your Results and Identify Where You Need Coaching
- Copyright ©–Mulligan 2016

The Career Planning Assessment helps you identify where you need grow an d manage your own career. You will be asked to rate your need for help l on 100 career items. These items are broken down into the six career management modules below. Each module will be further broken down by six topics.

- Career Transitioning
- Career Selection
- Career Preparation
- Career Placement
- Career Advancement
- Career Fulfillment.

The reason that most individuals do a poor job of planning their career is that they are unconsciously incompetent about planning their career. In other words, "they don't know enough about career planning to realize what they don't know."

Dr. Abraham Maslow stated that there are *four stages of competency* development. The four stages are outlined below.

*Stage Four-Unconsciously Competent-*You can perform the task without thinking about it. An expert on the topic-could coach others-able and willing

Stage Three-Consciously Competent- Know what you don't know about doing the task but not skillful yet to execute it. You are going through the process of learning until you can execute the task without thinking about it. Able but not quite willing to do it on your own.

*Stage Two-Consciously Incompetent-*You know what you need to improve and beginning the learning process. Willing to be coached but not able to do task.

Stage One- Unconsciously Incompetent- You don't know what you don't know-no knowledge of the fact that this is a task you need to do. Not willing and able to perform a specific task.

By participating in the survey, you will be able to rate your need to know level on 100 career topics. You will identify what you need to know in order to better plan your career. Once you identify the career topics where you need help or more information, you will have the option of obtaining help from your mentor, advisor or a career counselor.

INSTRUCTIONS:

COMPLETING THE CAREER PLANNING ASSESSMENT ©

This assessment survey is a data-gathering technique useful in identifying what you need to know to manage your career throughout your life. **Copyright ©–Mulligan 2012**

A. Read each of the 100 statements and consider your answer carefully before answering.
B. We will use the following *need to know* rating scale.
  6- Urgent Need to Know
  5- Strong Need to Know
  4- Moderate Need to Know
  3- Minimum Need to Know
  2- No Need to Know
  1- Expert on Topic

C. Mark the number that best represents your need to know and add up scores for each topic..
  (Assessing What You Know and Need to Know to Manage Your Career)

Career Transitioning Topic   **Total Score for 1 - 5 _____**
I need:
1. to know how to place myself in positions that are the right fit and offer the right rewards.
  ____6____5____4____3____2____1
2 to know how to identify a long range career target and place myself in positions that will help me reach my career target
  ____6____5____4____3____2____1
3. to know what I value in life so I can make career decisions that will make me happy.
  ____6____5____4____3____2____1
4. to know how to develop and execute a career pathing & management model that can help me manage my career until I want to retire.
  ____6____5____4____3____2____1
5. to know if I have the capability, knowledge, personality, financial means and business idea to be self employed.(owner of my own business or franchise.)
  ____6____5____4____3____2____1

Career Selection: Self Awareness Topic   **Total Score for 6 - 5 _____**
I need:
6.to know my interests and capabilities so I can establish realistic career objectives.
  ____6____5____4____3____2____1
7.to know my personality so I can place myself in career situations that are the right fit.
  ____6____5____4____3____2____1
8.to know my academic strengths and weaknesses so I can transform my weak academic areas into strengths and choose the right college major/career path that matches my strengths.
  ____-6____5____4____3____2____1
9.to know my personal values (who am I?) and work values (what do I want from work?) so I can place myself in positions that meet my values.
  ____6____5____4____3____2____1
10.to know my natural skills and those I have acquired through my work and educational experiences so I can select career positions where my skills are a good fit.
  ____6____5____4____3____2____1

60

6- Urgent Need to Know   5- Strong Need to Know   4- Moderate Need to Know
3- Minimum Need to Know   2- No Need to Know   1- Expert on Topic

Career Selection: Career Awareness Topic   Total Score for 6 -10 _____
I need:

11. to know the world of work: career fields(industries), functional areas, the many
career positions listed in the *Occupational Handbook* & career definitions.
_____6.____5 _____4 _____3 _____2 _____1
12. to know and understand the differences between the various work sectors.-public
sector (government, stock traded companies & schools) vs non-profits vs the private sector
(privately owned companies and private educational institutions)-pay, benefits, culture, work
pace, tenure, chances for advancement and retirement opportunities.
_____6____5 _____4 _____3 _____2 _____1
13.to know how to identify the career fields and positions that interest me and offer the
best opportunities for employment.
_____6____5 _____4 _____3 _____2 _____1
14.to know how to establish and conduct a low stress/informational interview with people
employed in my high-interest areas or companies where I might want to be employed.
_____6____5 _____4 _____3 _____2 _____1

15. to know how to find business data bases that can tell me about industries, companies and
hiring executives so I know what people and companies to research.

_____6____5 _____4 _____3 _____2 _____1

Career Preparation: Courses, Seminars, Internships Topic -Total Score 16 - 20 _____
I need:

16. to know about the various college courses, majors and graduate/professional programs and
how they will help me obtain my targeted career position.
_____6____5 _____4 _____3 _____2 _____1
17. to know the meaning of the ACT tests of educational development so I know my academic
strengths and weaknesses (English, math, science, social studies/reading) . I can then use this
information to obtain tutoring so I do well on the GRE, GMATS, LSAT, and MCAT later if I
decide to go to graduate or professional school.
_____6____5 _____4 _____3 _____2 _____1
18. to know how to sign up for and take skill building courses on time management, study habits,
a foreign language, computers/recent technology, sales, leadership and management, and human
relations etc. that will help me compete in the world of work.
_____6____5 _____4 _____3 _____2 _____1
19. to know how to obtain internships or part-time jobs in my chosen field to gain
experience, build my skills, knowledge and network to be hired in a full time position.
_____6____5 _____4 _____3 _____2 _____1
20. to know and understand what colleges, seminars, workshops and short courses will prepare
me for my future targeted position or present position.
_____6____5 _____4 _____3 _____2 _____1

61

Career Preparation: Academic Programs (A-C) - Agriculture, Architecture, Business and Communications Topic   Total Score for 21 - 25_____

I need:

21. to know related jobs and how to prepare for a career in **agriculture science/forestry**. (agricultural business, agricultural economics, agricultural mechanic, agriculture. production/tech., agronomy, animal sciences, farm & ranch management, fish game wildlife mgmt., food sciences/engineering, forestry & related science., horticulture ornamental horticulture., natural resources mgt., agriculture & agriculture tech.)

_____6 ____5 _____4 _____3 _____2 _____1

22. to know jobs and how to prepare for a career in **architecture/environmental science**. (architectural drafting, architecture, bldg. construction science, city/community./regulation planning, environmental design, interior design, landscape architecture, architecture. & environmental design.)

_____6 ____5 _____4 _____3 _____2 _____1

23. to know related jobs and how to prepare for a **career in business and management.** (accounting, banking and finance, business administration, business economics, city mgmt., hotel/restaurant mgmt., institutional mgmt., insurance and risk mgmt., international business mgmt., labor/human resources, management info systems, marketing mgt., organization behavior, human resources, real estate, small business mgmt., trade and industrial mgmt., transformation mgmt.)

_____6 ____5 _____4 _____3 _____2 _____1

24. to know related jobs and how to prepare for a career in **business and office mgt.** (bookkeeping/accounting. technology., business department./computer operations., court reporting, office supervision & management., secretarial, typing & general office, word processing, business & office, general)

_____6 ____5 _____4 _____3 _____2 _____1

25. to know related jobs and how to prepare for a career **communications and communications technology.**
(advertising, graphic commercial art, graphic & print communication, journalism, photo/film/video tech., motion pictures, news media, print media, public relations, radio/TV broadcasting, radio/TV product & technology communications. & communication technology, TV cable, video, radio)

_____6 ____5 _____4 _____3 _____2 _____1

Career Preparation: Academic Programs(C- F) -Community Service, Computers, Education, Engineering, Foreign Languages Topic-   Total Score for 26 - 30_____

26. to know jobs and how to prepare for a career in **community and personal services**. (corrections, cosmetology/hairstyling, criminal justice/criminology., fire protect/safety tech., funeral services./mortuary science., law enforcement & admin., library science./lib. assisting, military science/tech., parks & recreation, public administration, public affairs, social work, community & personal services.)

_____6 ____5 _____4 _____3 _____2 _____1

27. to know related jobs and how to prepare for a career in **computer and information science.**
(computer programming, computer science, data processing, info. science & systems,
math/computer science, computer & information, software design, website design)

_____6 _____5 ____4 _____3 _____2 _____1

28. to know related jobs and how to prepare for a career in **education & teacher education**.
(agricultural education, art education, business education, English education, foreign language
education., health education, human/family./cons. Science. Education., industrial arts education,
mathematics education, music education, physical education, science education, social
studies/social science education., special education, speech correction education., teaching
English as 2nd language, tech/trade & industrial education., teacher education other.)

_____6 ____5 ____4 ____3 _____2 _____1

29. to know related jobs and how to prepare for a career in **engineering/related technology**.
(aerospace engineering, agricultural engineering, architectural engineering, bioengineering &
bio-med. eng., ceramic engineering, chemical engineering, civil engineering, computer
engineering, construction eng./mgt., electrical. & electronic eng., engineering management,
engineering physics, engineering science, environmental health eng., geological & geophysics
eng., industrial engineering, materials engineering, mechanical engineering metallurgical
engineering, mining. & mineral eng., naval architecture. & marine eng., nuclear engineering,
ocean engineering, petroleum engineering, systems engineering, engineering, aeronautical
technology, ac/heating/refrigeration. Tech., architectural design tech., biomedical equipment
tech., civil engineering tech., computer engineering tech., construction/bldg. tech., drafting &
design tech., electrical eng. Technology, electronic eng., technology, electromechanical,
industrial. Tech. industrial. Production tech., laser/fiber-optic tech., manufacturing technology,
mechanical eng. Tech., mining & petroleum tech., packaging, occupational safety. & mapping
tech., surveying & mapping tech., engineering tech other, engineering related tech.)

_____6 ____5 ____4 ____3 _____2 _____1

30. to know related jobs and how to prepare for a career in the **foreign languages**.
 (Asiatic languages, classical languages, Chinese, French, German, Italian, middle eastern
languages, Russian, Spanish)

_____6 ____5 ____4 ___3 ____2 _____1

63

Career Preparation: Academic Programs (H-S)- Health, Human/Family, Laser Tech., Liberal Arts, Sales and Marketing Topic   Total Score for 31 through 35_____
I need:

31. to know related jobs and how to prepare for a career in **health & allied health fields** (chiropractor, dental assisting, dental hygiene, dental lab, dentistry, emergency med tech, health care administration., medical surgery assistant, medical lab technology, medical records, medicine-medical doctor, mental health, nursing, occupational therapy, optometry, pharmacy, physician assisting, radiology, rec./art/music therapy, veterinarian).
_____6 ____5 ____4 ____3 ____2 ____1

32. to know related jobs and how to prepare for a career in the **human and family field..** (child development/care/guidance, child care aide/assisting, culinary arts, family/consulting resource mgmt., fashion design, food production./management, food science. Nutrition./dietetics, human environment. & housing, individual & family development, textiles and clothing, human/family)
_____6 ____5 ____4 ____3 ____2 ____1

33. to know related jobs and how to prepare for a career in **laser/fiber-optic technology** (manufacturing technology, mechanical eng. Tech., mining & petroleum tech., occupational. Safety. & mapping tech., surveying & mapping tech., engineering tech, general)
_____6 ____5 ____4 ____3 ____2 ____1

34. to know related jobs and how to prepare for a career in the **humanities, letters, math, philosophy/religion**
(classics, comparative literature, creative writing, English general, linguistics, literature English/American, speech & rhetorical study, letters general, actuarial sciences, applied mathematics, statistics, mathematics general, bible studies, psychology, philosophy, religion, religious education, religious music, theology, philosophy./religion./theology.)
_____6 ____5 ____4 ____3 ____2 ____1

35. to know how to prepare for a career in **marketing/sales/distribution/logistics.** (advertising, fashion merchandising, retailing & sales, travel services & tourism, marketing & distribution, manufacturing, sports)
_____6 ____5 ____4 ____3 ____2 ____1

Career Preparation; Academic Programs- (S-V) Sciences, Study Overseas, Social Sciences, Trades, Visual/Performing Arts Topic   Total Score for 36 – 40_____
I need:
36. to know related jobs and how to prepare for a career in the **sciences.**
(astronomy, biology, earth science, geology, microbiology, oceanography, physics, zoology)
_____6 ____5 ____4 ____3 ____2 ____1

37. to know how to prepare for a career by taking a **study overseas program**.
_____6 ____5 ____4 ____3 ____2 ____1

38. to know how to prepare for a career in the **social sciences/pre-law** area.
(anthropology, economics, geography, history, international relationships, law, police
 science, political science/government, psychology, sociology, urban studies)
_____6 _____5 _____4 _____3 _____2 _____1

39. to know how to prepare for a career in the **trades and industrial fields** .
(aircraft technician, airplane piloting and navigation, automotive body repair, automotive
technology, aviation mgt., computer electronics, construction trades, diesel mechanics, drafting,
electrical equipment repair, heating/air condition/refrigeration. mech., machine
technology, mechanical drafting, welding and welding tech.)
_____6 _____5 _____4 _____3 _____2 _____1

40. to know related jobs and how to prepare for a career in the **visual/performing arts.**
(applied design, art, art history, cinematography/film/video, dance, drama/theatre,
entertainment, graphics arts and design, music and music composition and photography)
_____6 _____5 _____4 _____3 _____2 _____1

**Career Preparation- Functional Areas (E- H)- Educators, Engineering/Science,
Finance/Accounting/General Management, Human Resource Management Topic
Total Score for 41 through 45_____**
I need:
41. to know related jobs and how to prepare for a career as an **educator**.
(College or University President, Dean, Superintendent, Principal, Department
 Head, Curriculum Director, special education, counselor, professor, elementary teacher,
 junior high teacher, high school teacher, corporate trainer and professional coach.)
_____6 _____5 _____4 _____3 _____2 _____1

42. to know related jobs and how to prepare for a career in **engineering, research &
development and science.**
_____6 _____5 _____4 _____3 _____2 _____1

43. to know related jobs and how to prepare for a career in **finance and accounting**.
(CFO, budgeting, cost control, cash management, financing and managing of funds, portfolios,
credit, collection, taxes, and mergers/acquisitions, venture capital, private equity
_____6 _____5 _____4 _____3 _____2 _____1

44. to know related jobs and how to prepare for a career in **general management.**
(President/CEO, supervisor, middle management, senior management, Chief Level Officers,
Principal & Superintendent of Schools)
_____6 _____5 _____4 _____3 _____2 _____1

45. to know related jobs and how to prepare for a career in **human resource management.**
(Chief Human Resource Officer, employee relations, benefits, compensation, staffing, talent
management, management development, change management).
_____6 _____5 _____4 _____3 _____2 _____1

Career Preparation- Functional Areas (I-S) Informational Technology, Manufacturing, Materials Management, Medical/HealthCare, Sales/Marketing Topic
Total Score 46 to 50_____

46. to know related jobs and how to prepare for a career in **information technology**.
(CIO, V.P.-MIS, system analysis & design, software development, systems integration & implementation, support, and network administration)
_____6 _____5 _____4 _____3 _____2 _____1

47. to know related jobs and how to prepare for a career in **manufacturing.**
(product development, production engineering, planning, scheduling, and control,   automation, robotics, plant management, quality, and productivity.)
_____6 _____5 _____4 _____3 _____2 _____1

48. to know related jobs and how to prepare for a career in **materials management.** (purchasing, inventory management, materials and requirement planning, physical distribution, traffic and transportation, logistics and packaging.)
_____6 _____5 _____4 _____3 _____2 _____1

49. to know related jobs and how to prepare for a career in **medical/healthcare**.
(physicians, nurses, allied health- chiropractors, therapists, psychologists-,administration)
_____6 _____5 _____4 _____3 _____2 _____1

50. to know related jobs and how to prepare for a career in **sales and marketing.**
(advertising, sales promotion, marketing, product research, marketing management, sales and sales mgt., direct mail, telemarketing, customer service, and public relations).
_____6 _____5 _____4 _____3 _____2 _____1

Career Placement; Marketing Materials Topic   Total Score for 51 - 55_____
I need:

51. to know the various resume formats and how to write resumes for my targeted positions.
_____6 _____5 _____4 _____3 _____2 _____1

52. to know how to keep a resume updated from college through retirement keeping track of employers, positions, responsibilities and accomplishments.
_____6 _____5 _____4 _____3 _____2 _____1

53. to know how to write effective letters and emails to individuals who can hire me or help me get in front of people who can hire me.
_____6 _____5 _____4 _____3 _____2 _____1

54. to know how to use various online programs to market myself.
_____6 _____5 _____4 _____3 _____2 _____1

55.to know how to develop a one page personal profile and a business card that can be use in place of the resume to sell me.
_____6 _____5 _____4 _____3 _____2 _____1

Career Placement: Obtaining Interviews Topic   Total Score for 56 - 60_____

I need:

56. to know how to identify hiring managers in companies and conduct a control blitz that can get me into the company to meet the hiring manager.

____6 ____5 ____4 ____3 ____2 ____1

57. to know how to build an active networking team (through linkedin, facebook, my college/university, fraternity, neighborhood, church, friends, colleagues, past bosses etc.) and motivate these individuals to give me names of those who can meet with me and provide job leads or hire me

____6 ____5 ____4 ____3 ____2 ____1

58. to know the appropriate websites that can help me find job openings and obtain interviews.

____6 ____5 ____4 ____3 ____2 ____1

59. to know how to identify and contact recruiters that are searching for people in my field and at my compensation level.

____6 ____5 ____4 ____3 ____2 ____1

60. to know how to develop a job search action plan and tracking system that can tell me what I am doing right to produce interviews.

____6 ____5 ____4 ____3 ____2 ____1

Career Placement: Obtaining Offers through Effective Interviewing Topic
Total Score for 61 - 65_____

I need:

61. to know how to research a company and use the information to sell myself during the interview.

____6 ____5 ____4 ____3 ____2 ____1

62. to know how to prepare myself for two types of interviews- the low stress (exploratory-informational) and high stress (competing for a real job) interview.

____6 ____5 ____4 ____3 ____2 ____1

63. .to know the "knock-out" factors of an interview-how to establish rapport with the interviewer and the do's and don'ts-of interviewing.

____6 ____5 ____4 ____3 ____2 ____1

64 to know how to answer and ask appropriate questions during the interview so I sell myself.

. ____6 ____5 ____4 ____3 ____2 ____1

65. to use audio-video equipment to transform myself into a unconsciously competent interviewee.

____6 ____5 ____4 ____3 ____2 ____1

Career Placement: Follow-up and Negotiations Topic   – Total Score for 66 - 70_____

I need:

66. to know how to write a follow-up letter and sell myself to a company after the interview.

____6 ____5 ____4 ____3 ____2 ____1

67. to know how to prepare my references on what to say after a high stress interview.

____6 ____5 ____4 ____3 ____2 ____1

68. to know how to prepare for a second and third interviews, if necessary.

     ____6   ____5   ____4   ___3   ____2   ____1

69. to know how to negotiate compensation, a location package and other benefits without losing the offer

     ____6   ____5   ____4   ____3   ____2   ____1

70.   to know how to hold off one job offer while interviewing for other positions.

     ____6   ____5   ____4   ____3   ____2   ____1

Career Advancement: Transitioning from for One Company to Another Topic
Total Score for 71 through 75_____

I need:

71. to know when my career advancement has hit a wall and it is time to either move to another position in the same company or to another company.

     ____6   ____5   ____4   ____3   ____2   ____1

72. to know how to prepare for an employee downsizing -asking for a severance package when being dismissed, one that includes so many months of pay, health insurance, an outplacement service and unemployment pay.

     ____6   ____5   ____4   ____3   ____2   ____1

73. to know how to handle separation trauma when dismissed from the company and the stress of a job search that goes longer than expected.

     ____6   ____5   ____4   ____3   ____2   ____1

74. to know how to develop a story on why I left the company, one that puts me and the company in a positive light-never seen as burning bridges.

     ____6   ____5   ____4   ____3   ____2   ____1

75. to know how to choose and work closely with references to obtain my next position.

     ____6   ____5   ____4   ____3   ____2   ____1

Career Advancement – Career Pathing Strategy Topic- Total Score for 76 -80_____

I need:

76.- to know how to develop a Partnership Expectation PAC with my boss so we know what to expect from each other and what we need to accomplish during a time period.

     ____6   ____5   ____4   ____3   ____2   ____1

77. to know how to develop career pathing strategies and a career management model that can help me advance my career.

     ____6   ____5   ____4   ____3   ____2   ____1

78. .to know how to keep records on my work accomplishments so I can continually update my resume and wave my flag to increase promotional opportunities.

     ____6   ____5   ____4   ____3   ____2   ____1

79.to know what credentials (degrees and certifications) , experience and capabilities I need to acquire to advance my career.

     ____6   ____5   ____4   ____3   ____2   ____1

80.to know how to find career coaches and mentors throughout my career and work with them to develop and implement a career pathing strategy.

     ____6   ____5   ____4   ____3   ____2   ____1

6- Urgent Need to Know   5- Strong Need to Know   4- Moderate Need to Know
3- Minimum Need to Know   2- No Need to Know   1- Expert on Subject©

Career Advancement – Working with Others & Position Planning Topic
Total Score for 81 through 85_____
I need:
81. to know how to work with colleagues and a boss who is another gender, race or much younger or older.

_____6 _____5 _____4 _____3 _____2 _____1

82. to know how to sell my boss on implementing a talent and performance management system that will make everyone in the department the best or leaders in their field.

_____6 _____5 _____4 _____3 _____2 _____1

83. to know how to set an ultimate career objective and identify and put myself in the positions that will get me to my dream job.

_____6 _____5 _____4 _____3 _____2 _____1

84. to know the many things and behaviors that can derail my career.

_____6 _____5 _____4 _____3 _____2 _____1

85.to know and understand when the peter principle applies to me (This principal tells you that you have reached your level of competency on the job and cannot move forward without more credentials, preparation and experience.)

_____6 _____5 _____4 _____3 _____2 _____1

Career Fulfillment – Meeting Your Needs and Wants Topic
Total Score for 86 through 90_____
I need:
86.. to know if I am on the route career route at this time in my life (being in the right career situation- my present position is the right fit and the rewards are very satisfying).

_____6 _____5 _____4 _____3 _____2 _____1

87. to know what is satisfying and dissatisfying to me in my present work environment and position and make the adjustments to be happy.

_____6 _____5 _____4 _____3 _____2 _____1

88 .to know what it means to reach a self actualization state on the job and to evaluate where I am today on the self actualization scale.

_____6 _____5 _____4 _____3 _____2 _____1

89. to know if I am honoring my personal values and meeting my work values.

_____6 _____5 _____4 _____3 _____2 _____1

90. to know how to develop and execute a plan that will help me get on the right career route, be more satisfied and fulfilled with my work and obtain what I want from work.

_____6 _____5 _____4 _____3 _____2 _____1

Career Fulfillment: Helping Others Topic   **Total Score for 91 - 95**_____

    I need:

91. to know about programs that can elevate my human relations and helping skills so
I can build rapport and be more helpful to people at work, my family and friends.

     ____5   ____4   ____3   ____2   ____1

92. to know how I can balance my work and personal life so I can focus more on family
members, friends and people outside of work who need help.

     ____5   ____4   ____3   ____2   ____1

93. to know and understand how I can be a happier person. It is hard to reach out to others when
I am always focused on me and not in a pleasant state of mind.

     ____5   ____4   ____3   ____2   ____1

94. to know how to develop and execute a plan (the various ways) to help others.

     ____5   ____4   ____3   ____2   ____1

95. to know how I can work with my company/organization to build a helping/caring
culture- identifying where we can be more helpful to customers, fellow employees and the
people in the local community and put a plan into action.

     ____5   ____4   ____3   ____2   ____1

Career Fulfillment: Working with Your Boss/Colleagues Topic
Total Score for 96 through 100____

I need:

96. to know how to develop a working relationship with my present boss and future bosses.

     ____6   ____5   ____4   ____3   ____2   ____1

97. to know how to work with my boss to place him/her and myself on the right career route.

     ____6   ____5   ____4   ____3   ____2   ____1

98. to know how to work with my boss to promote our team unit within the organization and our
industry.

     ____6   ____5   ____4   ____3   ____2   ____1

99. to know how to develop a strong working relationship with my colleagues and others in the
organization.

     ____6   ____5   ____4   ____3   ____2   ____1

100. to know how to work with colleagues to build team cohesiveness, bring out the best in each
other too advance everyone's career and make work more rewarding and fulfilling.

     ____6   ____5   ____4   ____3   ____2   ____1

Identify Where You Need to Improve as a Career Manager

Place your total scores for each of the six career management modules and the topics under each of the six modules below. Check off the career planning modules and topics where you are weakest and circle your strengths. Then seek some coaching to improve yourself as a career planner and manager.

The Five Career Planning Modules   **Total Scores**

1.Career Transitioning   (One Topic)
Identifying Positioning-   Items 1-5
                                 Section Total Score   _____

2. Career Selection   (Three Topics)
Self Awareness –   Items 6-10
Career Awareness -   Items 11-15
                                 Section Total Score   _____

3. Career Preparation   (Seven Topics)
Courses, Seminars, Internships   Items 16-20   _____
Academic Programs- A to C   Items 21-25   _____
Academic Programs- C to F   Items 26-30   _____
Academic Programs- H to S   Items 31-35   _____
Academic Programs- S to V   Items 36-40   _____
Functional Areas-   E-H   Items 41-45   _____
Functional Areas-   I-S   Items 46-50   _____
                                 Section Total Score   _____

4. Career Placement   (Four Topics)
Marketing Materials   Items 51-55   _____
Sales & Marketing Campaign   Items 56-60   _____
Interviewing and Phone Skills   Items 61-65   _____
Follow Up and Negotiating   Items 66-70   _____
                                 Section Total Score _____
5. Career Advancement   (Three Topics)
Transitioning From Companies   Items 71-75   _____
Career Pathing Strategies   Items 76-80   _____
Position Planning   Items 81-85   _____
                                 Section Total Score   _____

6. Career Fulfillment   (Three Topics)
Meeting Your Needs   Items 86-90   _____
Helping Others   Items 91-95   _____
Working with Boss/Colleagues   Items 96-100   _____

Section Total Score   _____

Task Two
Learn the *Route 56 Career Management Model* Which Can Help You Manage Your Career from College to Retirement

The *Route 56 Career Management Model* was created to help individuals chart and manage their career journey. The <u>*first 5*</u> in the Model means you should plan your career out no more than five years at a time. You should develop a yearly growth plan and if properly executed, you should not be the same person in 5 years that you are today.

You live to grow and you grow by acquiring experience, knowledge, degrees, credentials and skills. This growth can place us in positions that we never thought we could occupy when in high school, college and while in our 20's and 30's. For example, Barack Obama probably never dreamed of being President of the United States but by obtaining his law degree from Harvard and being elected as a United States Senator, it gave him the opportunity to be elected President.

This means if you develop and execute a yearly career pathing and growth plan looking five years ahead, you will develop plans that can eventually put you in a career position that you never dreamed you could obtain. Abraham Maslow's self actualization theory states man wants to become and be.

(Example Rolling Five Year Ongoing Plans-But Not Necessarily like Below)

13 to 18	19 to 23	24 to 28	29 to 33	34 to 38	39 to 43	44 to 48	49 to 53	54 to 58	59 to 63+

The <u>*6*</u> represents six career management modules that you should be focusing each year as you move forward in your career. You set a growth objective for each of the five modules listed below and develop action plans to meet each objective.

1..Career Transitioning
- Moving through five growth stages- starting, advancement, peaking, uncertainty and semi-retirement or moving through this cycle two or three times due to career change
- Working in more than 10 to 15 jobs and for more than five organizations
- Learning how to deal with change
- Continuously charting your career or being unemployed for a long time

2. Career Selection (Choosing the next career field and position that's right for you)
- Self Assessment – develop a *Career Potential Profile*
- Career Assessment – explore the world of work-industries and positions?
- Select an industry and positions that match your *Career Potential Profile.*

3. Career Preparation (Qualify yourself for your targeted career field and position)
   - Select and attend the right college or university
   - Take courses in college that prepare you for your chosen career field/ position(s)
   - Internships in career fields, co-op work, or part-time work
   - College graduation – A.A., A.S., B.A., B.S.
   - Graduate work, degrees and being certified in your field
   - On the Job Training-workshops, seminars, certification
   - Find a career mentor- someone who can help you grow and be successful

4. Career Placement (Job Search – Place yourself in your next targeted position)
   - Target career field and position
   - Write your resume and marketing letters based on your targeted position
   - Develop a job search sales and marketing plan
     (Networking, websites, direct mail, recruiters, support groups, job fairs)
   - Sharpen your interviewing and telephone skills
   - Develop your negotiating skills
   - Meet with hiring managers and executives and obtain an offer
   - Negotiate your offer
   - Integrate yourself into the company/organizations
   - Excel as a leader

5. Career Advancement (Becoming what you want to be)
   - Graduate from high school
   - Graduate from a college or university
   - Finish graduate/professional school
   - Start and move up the leadership and management ladder
   - Know the key factors to advancement
   - Obtain and work with a career mentor or executive coach
   - Build and be on high performance teams
   - Continually build your credentials
   - Develop and stay in touch with a network of leaders
   - Learn how to wave your flag
   - Continually execute the *Route 56 Career Management Model*
   - Know when you have peaked in your career field and position

6. Career Fulfillment (Meeting your needs and becoming the best in your field)
   - Meet your needs at work (survival, security, social needs, self-esteem)
   - Assess your work satisfaction and develop a plan to enjoy your work
   - Balance your life and work in order to get the most out of your life
   - Become and be the best in your field – an expert leader
   - Continually fill out the Route 66 Career Satisfaction Survey so you can place yourself on the right career route-the right fit and rewards

You should be aware of the *Five Career Growth Stages* most people experience. When planning and evaluating our career journey, many of us do not know where we should be in our career at a certain age. We have developed the following chart to illustrate where the average worker should be in their career growth at a certain age in their life. The illustration below shows the *Five Career Growth Stages* a normal person would take as he/she works for a number of organizations and companies and moves slowly up the career ladder. An exception would be the individual on a fast track with a company or one who start or buys a company early in his/her life, grows the company and sells it for a lot of money. Even though that person is financially secure, he/she can be in the uncertainty stage. What do I do next? Or the semi-retirement stage where you travel and help others in the world without a monetary gain. If you start a new career, it puts you back in the first stage of the cycle, the career starting stage.

Age Passages	Five Career Growth Stages
13 to 18 19 to 23 24 to 28	The Career Starting Stage
29 to 33 34 to 38 39 to 43	The Career Advancement Stage
44 to 48 49 to 53 54 to 58	The Career Peaking Stage
59 to 63	The Career Uncertainty Stage
64 Plus	The Career Semi-Retirement Stage

We will describe these stages in more detail on the following pages.

The **Career Starting Stage** generally includes 13 to 28 year olds. These individuals are trying to figure out where they are today, where they want to be tomorrow and how they are going to get there. They are trying to decide what career field to enter, what positions best fits them and how to prepare for their career field and position(s). They also want to know how to conduct a job search to obtain their desired career positions after graduation from college. Many parents allow their son or daughter to live at home while in their 20's which enables them to zigzag through a number of career fields to learn what they should eventually pursue. However, you might see individuals of all ages today in Stage One a number of times as they switch careers and start over to find new employment. ©

The **Career Advancement Stage** generally includes those individuals 29 to 43 years of age. These individuals want to be empowered and have more responsibility in their present job. They also want to be promoted in title when they think they are ready and be placed in positions that offer more status, power and pay. This group is continually asking themselves the following questions:

- Do I need an MBA, advanced degree, special credentials or certification to advance?
- Can I have a company senior executive mentor and meet with him or her frequently?
- Can I meet the performance expectations of my boss? Do I do have enough resources to be successful?
- Am I perceived as a high-potential and talented person by my boss and others in the company?
- Are my personal, professional and financial needs being met by my present company?
- Do I have a better chance of advancing my career by staying or leaving?

The majority of those in the career advancement group are now married, have children, own a house, and are starting to save for their children's college education. These individuals might have more going on in their lives than they can handle.

The **Career Peaking Stage** generally includes individuals 44 to 58 years of age. These employees are the team leaders, managers and expert specialists in the organization. They are the visionaries, strategists, the planners, and the ones that establish the company's culture and receive the highest compensation.

During this 14-year period, individuals will advance until they reach the highest level of competency. Employees who want to keep advancing must know when they have reached the top in their career path. People who take on jobs they cannot handle eventually find themselves in trouble and could possibly be fired. It is nice to see yourself as superman or superwoman, but you also must be realistic in taking on new positions or walking into situations where you cannot be successful. This stage calls for honest career decision making. On the other hand, many people are afraid to take risks and stay in positions that offer very little challenge.

The **Career Uncertainty Stage** generally includes those 58 to 63 years of age. The reason this phase is called the Career Uncertainty Phase is because schools, organizations and companies usually want this age group to leave or retire early to reduce costs. The individuals in this category usually know they are on thin ice. This group costs the company more in benefits and total compensation than any other group. Because these individuals can start taking money from their pension funds at 59 ½, it is tempting for many to leave their companies or organizations early. The problem is having health insurance coverage until one is 65 and not spending your savings too early in life. Unless individuals in this age group own a business, occupy a professional position (MD., Dentist, Lawyer, etc.) or have a special skill a company really needs, they are vulnerable. Each person in this group should have a transition plan in place and execute the plan when it is the right time to leave. If a person in this group can start their own business and succeed, they could work longer.

The **Career Semi-Retirement Stage** generally includes those individuals 64 and over. People in this group still want to work for pay but not 50 to 70 hours per week. They would like to work 20 to 30 hours per week and have free time to travel and be with family and friends. This group wants to keep working to challenge their minds, use their talent, supplement their income and feel like they are contributing to society. Individuals in the *Uncertainty and Semi-Retirement Stages* should look at their avocations or passions (hobbies, special interests, etc.) and build a small business from their avocations. They might also think of doing team teaching in a junior, senior high school or community college, or be a part-time executive coach and mentor for employees in their former company. ©

The exceptions are those individuals who change careers two or three times in their lives. They will probably go through all five-growth phases in each career. For example, a person who starts a business at 28 and then sells it for 10 million dollars at age 35 would have gone through all five career growth stages. Another example would include a person starting as a school teacher, leaving education to work for a corporation and then starting and managing his or her own company. Can you think of other people who have gone through the five career stages early in life and are now in the career starting stage again?

Task Three
Review the *15 Proven Career Strategies* and
Execute These Strategies as You Manage Your Career Journey

15 Proven Career Pathing Strategies ©

The following are 15 proven career pathing strategies that can help you manage a career path that is rewarding and right for you...

#1 –You should execute a career management plan like the Route 555 Career Management Model. You should develop and meet specific objectives for each of the five career management modules -career selection, preparation, placement, advancement and fulfillment. As you know, the career fields and position(s) you occupy in life will determine:

- Your self image and how others view you
- Your status in life
- The power you have at work, in your community and nation
- Where you live – country, state, community and neighborhood
- Your income, wealth and benefits
- Who you marry and how long you stay married
- The freedom and amount of time you can spend with family and friends
- Where you take your vacations and the exposure you can give your children
- Where your children go to school and who they have as friends
- How you qualify to help others and who you eventually become
- When and where you can retire

#2- You should know your academic capabilities and interests and take the educational programs that will help you enter the career field that best fits you. If you took the ACT, and scored a 25 or higher on each of the four tests of educational development (English, math, social science or natural science), this reveals your education development in this academic area is very solid and you should do well academically in this area. If you scored a 25 or higher on the composite, you should do well on the GRE for graduate school and other professional school entrance exams. If you scored 16 or below on one of the four tests, it reveals you might need a tutor for that subject.

 #3- You should find significant people that are willing to serve as a career counselor, coach or mentor each year during each of their five year career/life plans. These individuals can be a teacher, friend of the family, faculty advisor, counselor, your boss, a high level executive or outside consultant. You could also find a person recently retired in the career field you want to enter. Most people would enjoy serving as your mentor for a period of time. You can share your career management plan with them, gain feedback and implement the plan under their guidance and direction.

#4 – You should continually assess yourself throughout life understanding your needs, wants, interests, talent, academic and work potential, capabilities, skills, values while charting and managing your career path yearly while looking ahead five years from now. As you move through life, you might want to use some 360° surveys to learn how people view you. You can grow from the feedback and the information you receive about yourself. They say if there is too much of a difference in the way you see yourself and the way others see you, you might need to talk to a counselor.

#5 - You should continually be exploring career opportunities in and outside your organization as well as looking into self-employment. You will be gaining confidence, experience, new skills, and career information as you move forward. in your career. This growth can give you the courage to change jobs and move into positions you never thought you could obtain.

#6 - As you select a career field and the position you wants to fill, plan on taking the necessary courses and training that will qualify you. Education and training is the fastest way to advance your career. Research shows that the individuals with the highest degrees make the most money. However there are many millionaires that dropped out of college and obtained their education in other ways. Obtaining an education doesn't always mean obtaining a degree from college. You can learn through internships, on the job training, taking seminars, online courses and especially by having a good mentor.

The U.S. Census Bureau[8] did a survey in 2014 of the average yearly salaries of workers ages 18 and older based on educational degree. The results were:

Education	Average yearly salary
No high school	$20,734
High school diploma	$29,915
Bachelor's degree	$56,206
Advanced degree	$84,602

Listed below is a breakdown of household income in America. This survey was conducted by the U.S. Census Bureau[9] in 2014 and included 105,539,122 households.
"

- **Top 4.6%**   **$150,000 Plus**

- **Next 7.7%**   **$100,000 to $150,000**

- **Next 10.2%**   **$75,000 to $99,000**

- **Next 35.8%**   **$35,000 to $75,000**

- **Bottom 41.7%**   **Less than $35,000**

If you are born in the wealthiest families of America, you have a better chance of obtaining the top jobs. However, if you obtain an A.A., B.A., MBA or Ph.D., you give yourself a chance to climb the social economic ladder to the top. The contacts you make in college, your degree and the knowledge you learn are the "equalizers "to "moving up".

What was your household income when you were in high school?

$_____ Did your Mom and Dad both work?

What is your household income today?
$_____ What did you do to improve or hurt your situation?

What do you anticipate your household income to be in 15 years?
$_____Will one person in the family be working or more?

Will you have to hire a nanny in order to work? Or will you be the nanny?

#7 –You should try to save money throughout your career journey by investing in 401Ks, IRAs, real estate, other sound investment opportunities or obtaining stock options from your company. However, don't let materialism (satisfying the wants more than the needs) blind you and place you in financial shackles. It is difficult to shift careers or take a lesser paying position if you are trapped by the need of a high established income. Remember, you might make a high income now but your situation could change. The stock market goes up and down so be careful. I have . met clients who have lost millions and if the monthly cost of your life style is too high, you can be in trouble.

#8- If you marry, it is important you have a spouse that wants to take part in your career decision making process and support you. People change as they move through life passages. Hopefully you and your spouse will always be there for one another. The U.S. Census Bureau[10] conducted a 30 year study in 2014 to find out the median age of males and females marrying.

The results are listed below.

1970		2014	
Women	20.8	Women	25.3
Men	23.2	Men	27.1

How do you see a spouse impacting your career path? We have seen many clients turn down excellent jobs out of Chicago because their spouse refused to move. We have also seen clients move to out of the way places to please their spouse.

#9 –You need to learn how to write an effective resume and job search sales and marketing plan and keep both up to date. You should target a specific career field and position and try to obtain as many interviews as possible. Job offers will eventually come based on how well you interview. You should be interviewed using audio video equipment so you can see how you come across to others.

#10 You should start building career advancement networking teams in college and continue building these network teams throughout your career. You can start with eight students in your undergraduate major, fraternity or sorority and then build other networking teams in graduate school and future work situations. These teams can stay together throughout everyone's life and help each other in job searches and career advancement. You can use Linkedin, Twitter, e-mail or set up your own system to stay in touch.

#11. Your should continually assess the career route you are on by using *The Route 66 Career Satisfaction Survey*. You need to develop and execute action plan(s) and tasks that will improve your situation in each position. Mulligan & Associates can furnish this survey.

Psychologist Frederick Herzberg[11] conducted many studies on the satisfying and unsatisfying elements in a work environment. His findings are below.

Satisfying elements related to job content

Achievements
Recognition
Work
} Good for short run

Responsibilities
Advancement
Challenge
Growth
} Good for long run

Satisfying elements related to job climate.

- Supervisor/manager
- Company policy and administration
- Interpersonal relations
- Salary
- Working conditions

ExecuNet[12], an organization that helps executives find positions, did a study in 2011 to research the job satisfaction of executives. Of the total 1498 respondents, 77% of the respondents said they plan to leave their job in the next 6 months and 61% were dissatisfied with their current job. 33% of the executives stated job frustration started from a lack of challenge, opportunity for advancement and personal growth. 13% cited the culture as a reason for leaving while 12% were in search of better compensation. Compensation was given as the top reason executives will jump ship to another company.

Other important factors were location, corporate culture, and personal growth experiences. Women gave the top marks for the same factors as men but rated improved work/life balance as high on their list.

#12-You should strive to work with your boss so both of you are successful. One suggestion would be to develop a Partnership Expectation Pac. Both of you should sit down and write out what you can expect from each other. This would include both work tasks and relationship building behaviors. You would then discuss the expectations and agree to them. Your boss at work, like your spouse, plays an extremely important role in your career path. You will have many bosses in your career journey so developing a Partnership Expectation PAC that is in writing will benefit both of you and your boss.. If your boss leaves, show the Partnership Expectation PAC to your new boss and rework it.

#13-With so much diversity in the workforce today, you should learn to be respectful, flexible, understanding and cooperative with members on your team. It's also important to your career if you can speak more than one language. Research shows that there is an increasing number of Hispanics in the workforce and a lot of companies do work in the Far East. Study the languages that are best for your career. Your teammates might be younger, older, or of another gender. However, everyone has the same goal and that is to be successful. Everyone needs to learn how to work together and help each other obtain what they want out of a career. Remember that you probably will not be working more than a year or two with your present team members so everyone should help each other grow and enjoy their work.

#14 –You should meet with your team mates and establish the mission of transforming your unit (department or division) and each other into the best in your fields. If you are a high performer and part of a winning team, your company will always want you to stay and other competing companies will want to recruit you.

#15 You can raise your level of happiness and be rewarded in your career journey if you can learn how to be a performance facilitator or helper to others. However, before a person can help others, they must bring out the best in themselves first. As you know, individuals need to strive to keep themselves mentally, physically, financially, spiritually, and socially sound. If you can become a healthy person and develop your helping skills, then you can help others.

What are some other strategies that you can use to be effective at work and advance your career and life journey?

Task Four
Develop, Execute and Meet a Growth Plan to
Become a Career Manager

In What Career Modules or Areas Do You Need to Improve to be an effective *Career Manager*? Rank Each of the Six Career Modules 1 to 5 with 5 being a Strong Need for Coaching and 1 Being a Weak Need for Coaching.

Career Transitioning- Review the Topic Items and Rank Need for Coaching

Career Selection- Review the Topic Items on Survey and Rank Need for Coaching.

Career Preparation- Review Topic Items on Survey and Rank Need for Coaching.

Career Placement-Review Topic Items on Survey and Rank Need for Coaching.

Career Advancement-Review Topic Items on Survey and Rank Need for Coaching.

Career Fulfillment- Review Topic Items on Survey and Rank Need for Coaching.

Special Note-
Take Steps to Manage Your Career

There are many students who graduate from college and still do not have a clear picture of what they want to do for a career. This is not uncommon with a lot of people today. Recently, we conducted a job search workshop at the Arlington Heights Library in Arlington Heights, Illinois. When we asked the 45 participants who were from 35 to 50 in age what the number one impediment was to them finding a job, they said we do not have a career field and position targeted. They did not know what position or career field to go after next. This says that most people want to join an organization or company and work in a particular position until they retire. They don't manage their career. They want someone to guide and take care of them. You might want to see a career counselor on campus to help you understand yourself and how you fit into the world of work. The following ten tasks will help you understand yourself and the world of work and asks you to develop a *Career Profile* based on the accumulated information to help your tentatively select a career field and college major. We will focus on *Self and Career Awareness* which is key to charting your career journey.

Step One-Self Awareness- Learn About Yourself
If you graduated from college and still need help in identifying a career path and what position you should go after, you should go to your local college counseling center for help or find a career counselor at home where you live. You probably need to go through some in-depth assessment and discuss your results with a consultant who can help you develop a career plan. *Tasks Three, Four and Five* of Goal Four will help you understand yourself.

Step Two-Career Awareness- Learn About the World of Work
Tasks One, Two, Six, Seven, Eight, Nine and 10 of Goal Four will define the world of work and what is happening in the world of work today.
Again, this information should help you

As previously mentioned, you can go to the local library and research careers in the online resources section. You can go to:
- Career Cruising- You can explore careers, education and training needed, employment guide for resumes, interviewing, and more.
- The Occupational Outlook Handbook-Reviews careers and occupations.
- Ferguson's Career Guidance Center- A comprehensive career research database
- Careers Internet Database-Comprehensive report on careers for the 21st Century-most up to date information.
- O*Net Online-The nation's primary source of occupational information.

Step Three-Build a *Career Profile* **and tentatively select a career field/path and a college major to pursue.**

Goal # Four-
Understand Career Pathing, Yourself and the World of Work and Tentatively Select a Career Field/Path and College Major to Pursue

Page

86   **Task One-** Understand the Definitions of Career Path, Career Field and Career Position

90   **Task Two-** Understand Why There is No Job Security Today

94   **Task Three-** Write Out Your Career Aspiration

96   **Task Four-** *Understand Yourself-* Rank Four Work Tasks and Relate Them to 26 Career Clusters

97   **Task Five-** *Understand Yourself-* Rate Your Strengths on 100 Skills

101   **Task Six-** *Understand the World of Work-*Review the 10 Groups of Industries Listed in the *Expanded Occupational Outlook Handbook*

109   **Task Seven-***Understand the World of Work-*Review the 115 Top Projected Career Positions until 2015 and Select Several That Appeal to You

112   **Task Eight-***Understand the World of Work-* Review the Majors Offered by Colleges and Universities and Select Several That Appeal to You.

116   **Task Nine-** *Understand the World of Work-*Learn How to Conduct an Exploratory or Informational Interview to Gain Information on Organizations, Industries and People

119   **Task Ten-***Understand the World of Work:* Learn about the Job Opportunities for College Graduates

122   **Task Eleven–** Build a *Career Profile* from the Information Accumulated and Select a Tentative Career Field and Major

Task One-
Understand the Definitions of Career Path, Career Field and Career Position.

A **career path** is succession of positions/jobs that a person has held in one or number of industries since he/she started working. The positions/jobs held could have been in one career field or a number of them. You need to study your career path, know where you have been and chart a career path that is most likely to provide you a future.. You need to know that once you have been in a particular career field/industry for a number of years, it is difficult to get off this path without going back to college, taking a pay cut or knowing someone who will hire you.

A **career path** also includes moving into management and advancing from being a supervisor to a senior executive or being in a non-management role operating as a salesperson, an accountant, a researcher, an engineer, a teacher, a retail clerk, or computer programmer, etc. and becoming an expert leader in your position. See management ladder chart below.

Level 1	CEO/President
Level 2	Chief Level Officers
Level 3	Senior Management – Vice Presidents
Level 4	Middle Management
Level 5	Supervisors

A **career field is an industry where you fill a position. Explore the industries below.**

CAREER FIELDS (INDUSTRIES)
THIS CLASSIFICATION SYSTEM IS BASED ON THE U.S. GOVERNMENT SIC CODES

00.0 **A.00**	**GENERALIST**	**I.00** **I.10**	**SERVICE INDUSTRIES** HOSPITALITY; INCLUDING HOTELS, RESORTS, CLUBS, RESTAURANTS, FOOD & BEVERAGE SERVICES
B.00	**AGRICULTURE, FORESTRY, FISHING, MINING**	**I.11**	ENTERTAINMENT, LEISURE, AMUSEMENT, RECREATION, SPORTS, TRAVEL
		I.12	MUSEUMS, GALLERIES, MUSIC/ARTS, LIBRARIES & INFORMATION SERVICES, MEMBERSHIP & OTHER NON-PROFITS
C.00	**CONSTRUCTION**	**I.13**	HIGHER EDUCATION
		I.14	PHARMACEUTICAL (OTHER THAN MANUFACTURING)
D.00	**MANUFACTURING INDUSTRIES**	**I.15**	LEGAL
D.10	**FOOD, BEVERAGE, TOBACCO & KINDRED PRODUCTS**	**I.16**	COMPUTER SERVICES
D.11	**TEXTILE, APPAREL, RELATED PRODUCTS**	**I.17**	ACCOUNTING & MISCELLANEOUS BUSINESS SERVICES

D.12	**LUMBER, WOOD, FURNITURE & FIXTURES**	**I.18**	**EQUIPMENT SERVICES, INCLUDING LEASING**
D.14	**PRINTING & ALLIED INDUSTRY**	**I.20**	**HUMAN RESOURCE SERVICES**
D.15	**CHEMICALS & ALLIED PRODUCTS**	**I.21**	**LAW ENFORCEMENT, SECURITY**
D.16	**SOAP, PERFUME, COSMETICS**		
D.17	**DRUGS, PHARMACEUTICALS**	**J.00**	**COMMUNICATIONS/MEDIA**
D.18	**MEDICAL DEVICES & INSTRUMENTS**	**J.10**	**ADVERTISING, PUBLIC RELATIONS**
D.19	**PLASTICS, RUBBER PRODUCTS**	**J.11**	**PUBLISHING, PRINT MEDIA**
D.20	**PAINTS, ALLIED PRODUCTS, PETROLEUM PRODUCTS**	**J.12**	**NEWS MEDIA (E.G. INTERNET, MULTIMEDIA)**
D.21	**LEATHER, STONE, GLASS, CONCRETE, CLAY PRODUCTS**	**J.13**	**TV, CABLE, MOTION PICTURES, VIDEO, RADIO**
D.22	**PRIMARY & FABRICATED METAL PRODUCTS**	**J.14**	**TELEPHONE, TELECOMMUNICATIONS**
D.23	**INDUSTRIAL MACHINERY & CONSUMER APPLIANCES**		
D.24	**TRANSPORTATION EQUIPMENT (E.G. AUTOMOBILES)**	**K.00**	**PUBLIC ADMINISTRATION/GOVERNMENT**
D.25	**COMPUTER EQUIPMENT & COMPONENTS**	**K.10**	**DEFENSE**
D.26	**CONSUMER ELECTRONICS**		
D.27	**TEST & MEASUREMENT EQUIPMENT**	**L.00**	**ENVIRONMENTAL SERVICES**
D.28	**MISCELLANEOUS MANUFACTURING INDUSTRIES**	**L.10**	**HAZARDOUS WASTE, STUDY, CLEAN UP**
E.00	**TRANSPORTATION**	**M.00**	**AEROSPACE**
		N.00	**PACKAGING**
F.00	**WHOLESALES TRADE**	**P.00**	**INSURANCE**
		Q.00	**REAL ESTATE**
G.00	**RETAIL TRADE**	**R.00**	**HIGH TECH**
		S.00	**SOFTWARE**
H.00	**FINANCE**	**T.00**	**BIOTECH/GENETIC ENGINEERING**
H.10	**COMMERCIAL BANKING**	**U.00**	**HEALTHCARE**
H.11	**INVESTMENT BANKING**	**V.00**	**NON-CLASSIFIABLE INDUSTRIES**
H.12	**SECURITIES & COMMODITIES BROKERS**		
H.13	**VENTURE CAPITAL**		
H.14	**OTHER FINANCIAL SERVICES**		

A **career position** is defined as the job title you held or now hold in an organization or industry. Each job has a description of the responsibilities and tasks that a person is expected to carry out with written performance standards that must be met. Jobs are classified as occupations by the U.S. Department of Labor[i]. http://online.onetcenter.org/

CAREER POSITIONS (FUNCTIONAL AREAS)

00.0	**GENERALIST**		06.0	**HUMAN RESOURCE MANAGEMENT**
			06.1	BENEFITS, COMPENSATION PLANNING
01.0	**GENERAL MANAGEMENT**		06.2	PERSONNEL SELECTION, PLACEMENT & RECORDS
01.1	DIRECTORS		06.3	TRAINING
01.2	SENIOR MANAGEMENT (E.G. CEO,COO, PRESIDENT, GENERAL MANAGER)			
01.3	MIDDLE MANAGEMENT		07.0	**FINANCE & ACCOUNTING**
01.4	ADMINISTRATIVE SERVICES		07.1	CFO's
01.5	LEGAL		07.2	BUDGETING, COST CONTROLS
			07.3	CASH MANAGEMENT, FINANCING & MANAGEMENT OF FUNDS, PORTFOLIOS
02.0	**MANUFACTURING**		07.4	CREDIT & COLLECTION
02.1	PRODUCT DEVELOPMENT		07.5	TAXES
02.2	PRODUCTION ENGINEERING, PLANNING, SCHEDULING & CONTROL		07.6	MERGERS & ACQUISITIONS
02.3	AUTOMATION, ROBOTICS		07.7	RISK MANAGEMENT
02.4	PLANT MANAGEMENT			
02.5	QUALITY		08.0	**INFORMATION TECHNOLOGY**
02.6	PRODUCTIVITY		08.1	MIS MANAGEMENT (E.G. CIO, VP-MIS)
			08.2	SYSTEMS ANALYSIS & DESIGN
03.0	**MATERIALS MANAGEMENT**		08.3	SOFTWARE DEVELOPMENT
03.1	PURCHASING, INVENTORY MANAGEMENT		08.4	SYSTEMS INTEGRATION/IMPLEMENTATION
03.2	MATERIALS & REQUIREMENT PLANNING		08.5	SUPPORT
03.3	PHYSICAL DISTRIBUTION, TRAFFIC & TRANSPORTATION, LOGISTICS		08.6	NETWORK ADMINISTRATION
03.4	PACKAGING		08.7	DATABASE ADMINISTRATION
04.0	**MEDICAL/HEALTHCARE**		09.0	**RESEARCH & DEVELOPMENT/SCIENTISTS**
04.1	PHYSICIANS			
04.2	NURSES		10.0	**ENGINEERING**
04.3	ALLIED HEALTH (E.G. CHIROPRACTORS, THERAPISTS, PSYCHOLOGISTS)			
04.4	ADMINISTRATION		11.0	**SPECIALIZED SERVICES**
			11.1	MANAGEMENT CONSULTANTS
05.0	**SALES & MARKTING**		11.2	MINORITIES
05.1	ADVERTISING, SALES PROMOTION		11.3	FUND RAISERS & OTHER NON-PROFIT SERVICES
05.2	MARKETING & PRODUCT RESEARCH		11.4	ENVIRONMENTALISTS
05.3	MARKETING MANAGEMENT		11.5	ARCHITECTS
05.4	SALES & SALES MANAGEMENT		11.6	TECHNICIANS
05.5	DIRECT MAIL, MARKETING, TELEMARKETING		11.7	ATTORNEYS
05.6	CUSTOMER SERVICE		11.8	GRAPHIC ARTISTS, DESIGNERS
05.7	PUBLIC RELATIONS		11.9	PARALEGALS
			12.0	**INTERNATIONAL**

Most positions in the world of work can be placed in three categories:

- The Laborers – People who do the work and service the customer
- The Management Team – People who manage the workers to see the business plan is executed and achieved.
- The Senior Management and Sales Team – People who establish the business to be in, set profit objectives, plans, budgets, and find the money and customers to stay in business.

You should go online and learn about the various industries.. Your next step would be to identify the industries and positions that appeal to you the most and set up an exploratory interview with some one that is in both the industry and position. You can go to the following on-line resources to learn more about career fields and positions.

- **career cruising**
- **occupational outlook handbook**
- **ferguson's career guidance center**
- **o*net online**

Task Two
Understand Why There is No Job Security Today

Prior to the mid-80's companies did not face the competitive challenges of today's organizations. The majority of workers worked for one or two companies their entire career. They depended on the organization to take care of them through the work years and into retirement with a good pension and health plan. Long-term strategies and succession planning were consistently part of the business agenda as multi-layers of management positions offered excellent advancement opportunities for everyone. Change was slow, anxiety was low and job security prevailed.

Three traditional career paths at that time are shown below.

	Ages 5-18	Ages 18-23	Ages 23-62	Ages 62+
Career Path One	School	College	Work	Retirement
Career Path Two	School	Military	Career change	Retirement
Career Path Three	School	Family management	Part-time work	Retirement

Career Pathing Today

More than at any time in history, we are living in an age of change. Major changes in our lives are more rapid, complex, turbulent and unpredictable and they are unlike any changes we have encountered before. We are in an era that is sweeping society into a massive transformation that will have a lasting effect on the workplace. It is estimated that there have been more structural changes in U.S. industry in the last five years than in the previous thirty. Continuous change, complexity, constraints and conflicts best characterize today's business environment. Major economic, technological, social, cultural and political forces are driving the way firms do business and how they position their resources.

One of the biggest challenges facing CEOs and their organizations is anticipating and managing change. CEOs are constantly talking about how to adjust to fast-moving changes, charting, comprehending and overcoming them. Oakleigh Thorne, Chief Executive Officer of C.C.H., Inc. was quoted in The Chicago Tribune as saying,"The place of change is so fast today that if you don't have your antenna up and aren't modifying your plans to react to the change, you are dead. Change is certain but progress is not."

New patterns of independence among governments, companies, unions, managers and workers are emerging, as we have become a world community. The business sector has become a global playing field without borders.

Of all the changes, the one that has affected companies the most is the pressure to generate higher earnings to increase shareholder value. Constant stress has come from the watchdog eyes and the voice of the investment analysis community, as well as stockholders. The daily stock market report is the most important news of the day. Millions of people want to know how their stocks are doing. Even the Federal government has considered putting Social Security funds into the stock market, which would put even more pressure on companies to increase earnings.

The marching orders for CEOs and Presidents are simple – hit your profit target or be gone. In essence, making money and satisfying stockholders today has become the number one priority. A recent *Chicago Tribune* (June 2008)[12] issue revealed the average time for a CEO in a Fortune 500 company is now two and one-half years.

Today's executives have a very short time span to increase shareholder value. This enormous pressure to increase earnings has forced many CEOs, presidents and senior management teams to take action steps that leaders in the earlier years never contemplated and it has impacted employment in America. Some of these action steps have included:

- Downsizing, restructuring and reengineering the workforce on a large scale.
- Continuously rightsizing on a small scale to cut expenses.
- Using advance technology to do more work with fewer people.
- Eliminating middle management positions and asking those remaining to take on more responsibility, work longer hours and do more with fewer resources.
- Outsourcing specific department areas such as IT, benefits, etc., to consulting firms.
- Eliminating the cost of benefits by hiring more temporary and part-time people.
- Issuing contracts to large national providers instead of local small businesses to cut more expenses.
- Acquiring or merging with other companies to increase sales and market share, and position the company as a leader in the industry.
- Moving manufacturing off shore to obtain less expensive labor.
- Moving away from research, development and manufacturing to find products produced by others.
- Asking those who remain with the company to take on two jobs
- Asking employees to take a cut in pay or take vacation without pay
- Tightening control on expenses to come in below budget.
- Taking longer to pay suppliers and vendors.
- Asking vendors to drop their prices which meant they would cut staff as well
- Making the retired and present employees pay more for their benefits.
- Providing incentives to motivate older workers to retire early.

The pressure and changes made to increase shareholder value has impacted everyone's career path in big and small companies and has caused much stress in the workforce. This stress has created:

- Insecurity (fear)
- Distrust (poor working relationships)
- Lack of focus (productivity)
- Organization paranoia (we vs. they)
- Low morale (poor attitude)
- Poor performance (meeting expectations)
- No commitment (purpose)
- Sickness (absenteeism)
- Fear of job loss (high anxiety)
- Burn-out (distress)
- Feeling of abandonment (analytic depression)
- Not being able to think and solve problems (stress/tension)
- A lack of loyalty (retention)
- A loss of experienced people (early retirement)

Today's Career Paths

Age				
70	*Retirement*	*Retirement*	*Retirement*	*Retirement*
65	Job change	Company change		
	Job change			
	Company change	Company change	Company change	
55	Job change	Job change	Job change	
	Company change	Job change	Job change	
	Job change	Job change	Job change	
45	Company change	Company change	Company change	
	Job change	Job change	Job change	
	Company change	Company change	Company change	
	New company	New company	Family management	Government/
35	Job change	Job change		Professional
	New company	New company		positions
	Graduate school	College	Job change	Self-Employed
25	Job change		New company	(Fewer
	Job change			changes)
18	College	Military	College	College
5	School	School	School	School

New patterns of independence among governments, companies, unions, managers and workers are emerging, as we have become a world community. The business sector has become a global playing field without borders.

Career Pathing and Change

We must remember that career decision making is an ongoing process. Career change will naturally occur due to the acquisitions of new skills, experience, self realization and information about career opportunities.

Ron Kutscher of the U.S. Department of Labor Bureau of Labor Statistics told Dr. Mulligan in 2010 " As people graduate from high school and college and begin establishing career goals, there is considerable zigzagging through occupational groups. The reason is that many individuals have no experience prior to taking the first job and once they get there, they discover it isn't what they want...We have found that one out of five workers were not in the same occupation they were in one year earlier. Part of this occupational movement reflects the dynamic labor market. The research of others reveals that the average employee will work for 10.5 employers in his or her lifetime, with one-third the employees eventually working for one employer an average of 15 years."

The above statement clearly points out that people are always searching for what meets their needs at the time. We are motivated and qualified for different positions at various times in our lives and we need to be ready to move to that next opportunity.

You Are In Charge Of Your Own Career Today – View Yourself as Self-Employed

We all know private and publicly traded companies strive to make profit and increase shareholder value. We hope companies who meet their profit objectives will reward all their stakeholders and not those who own a lot of stock in the company. However, in the end, it is still up to employees to chart a career path that is rewarding and right for them and be ready to conduct a job search and move from one company to another.

A major point to remember is that you can't depend on your organization or company to take care of you because there is too much change in management today. A person can have a different boss each year and most of them view their role as pushing you for production and results, not helping you with career pathing or giving you security.

Task Three
Write Out Your Career Aspiration

As you move through each of your five-year career transitioning stages, you might have the same career aspiration from age 15 to retirement. However, as we get older and gain more credentials and experience, we will go after positions we never thought we could obtain. Barack Obama is a good example of how one's career aspiration can change. There are 15 factors listed below that can impact your career decision making process. They are:

1) The family into which you are born – your parents' expectations of you
2) The success you have in school – level of educational achievement
3) Talent awareness through teachers, coaches and parents
4) The education, experience, skills and work knowledge you acquire (capabilities) and vision of what you can do in the world of work
5) The people you meet and know and how they influence you
6) Bosses at work and performance reviews
7) The career positions you obtained and how they prepared you for the next position.
8) Being security and survival oriented –not a risk taker
9) Your marital and children situation
10) Your personality (competitive vs. laid back)
11) The need to live in a certain location.
12) Your self-image and how others view you
13) How much you believe and have confidence in yourself.
14) Your work ethic– willing to work long hours and do what it takes to complete the job
15) The type of lifestyle you want to live-willing to pay the price for fame and fortune. ©

Please review the 15 factors and identify the main factors that are influencing your career aspiration at this time. If you can think of other factors, please list them.

My career aspiration in **high school** was to become a _____.
What factor(s) influenced your decision the most?

My career aspiration **now** is to become a _____
What factor(s) influenced your decision the most?

Harvard MBA. <u>vs</u> A Mexican Fisherman

You, your parents, professor or fellow students should read this story and discuss together what this story means to you in regard to planning your future career,

 A boat docked in a tiny Mexican village. An American tourist complimented the Mexican fisherman on the quality of his fish and asked him how long it took to catch them.

"Not very long," answered the Mexican. "But then why didn't you stay out longer and catch more?" asked the American. The Mexican explained that his small catch was sufficient to meet his needs and those of his family.

The American asked, "But what do you do with the rest of the time? "I sleep late, fish a little, play with my children, and take a siesta with my wife. In the evenings, I go into the village to see my friends, have a few drinks, play the guitar, and sing a few songs. I have a full life."

The American interrupted, "I have an MBA from Harvard and I can help you! You should start by fishing longer every day. You can then sell the extra fish you catch. With the extra revenue, you can buy a bigger boat. With the money the larger boat will bring, you can buy a second one and a third one and so on until you have an entire fleet of trawlers. Instead of selling your fish to a middle man, you can negotiate directly with the processing plants and maybe even open your own plant. You can then leave this little village and move to Mexico City, Los Angeles, or even New York City! From there you can direct your huge enterprise."

"How long would that take?" asked the Mexican. "Twenty, perhaps twenty-five years," replied the American. "and after that?"

"Afterwards? That's when it gets really interesting," answered the American, laughing. "When your business gets really big, you can start selling stocks and make millions!" "Millions? Really? And after that?"

"After that you will be able to retire, live in a tiny village near the coast, sleep late, play with your children, catch a few fish, take a siesta with you wife and spend your evenings drinking and enjoying your friends."

Do you want to be more like the fisherman or the Harvard MBA? Which of the characters are most like your parents? Can you work with your parents and take the path that truly reflects your take on work?

Task Four-
Understand Yourself- Rank Four Work Tasks and
Relate Them to 26 Career Clusters

Ranking and Relating Work Tasks to 26 Career Areas

One of the best ways to identify a career field to enter is to rank the work tasks that you enjoy and are best at doing.. Listed below are four work tasks that we do every day while working. Rank the four work tasks based on your interest and capability to do them.

1-highest and 4 lowest

_____**People** –ability to work with, help, amuse or influence the actions or thinking of people. (social skills, persuasive skills and leadership skills)

_____**Data**-ability to handle details, facts, figures, records, or files quickly and accurately (clerical skills, language usage, numerical skills and management skills)

_____**Things**-ability to operate, repair or build machinery or equipment or to understand how living or nonliving things function (mechanical reasoning, space relationships, advanced math, manual dexterity)

_____**Ideas**-ability to develop strategies, solve problems and express thoughts or feelings in inventive or artistic ways (creativity, problem solving, artistic)

The American College Testing Program, in developing their interest inventory, show the relationship of 26 career areas with four work tasks. Identify your number one ranked work task and then your top two and identify the career areas that best match your work tasks.

People –One Work Task
- Education
- Community Services
- Health Care
- Personal Services

Data-One Work Task
- Communications and Records
- Financial Transactions
- Regulation and Protection

Things –One Work Task
- Agriculture/Forestry
- Computer/Information Specialties
- Construction & Maintenance
- Crafts and Related
- Manufacturing & Processing
- Mechanical & Electrical Specialties

Ideas –One Work Task
- Applied Arts-Visual
- Medical Diagnosis & Treatment
- Medical Technologies
- Social Science

People & Data-Two Work Tasks
  *Employment Related Services
  *Marketing & Sales
  *Management

People & Ideas-Two Work Tasks
  *Applied Arts (visual and spoken)
  * Creative & Performing Arts

Data & Things-Two Work Tasks
  *Distribution & Dispatching
  *Transport Operations

Ideas & Things-Two Work Tasks
  * Engineering & Technologies
  *Natural Sciences & Technologies

(Permission given by American College Testing)

Task Five
Understand Yourself- Rate Your Strengths on 100 Skills

There are over 100 skills listed on the following three pages. Please review each skill and rate yourself in regard to the level you have mastered the skill. Use the following rating scale.

3. Mastered the skill   2. Somewhat mastered the skill   1. Not mastered the skill

List below those skills that you have mastered and then list the career areas or positions you think would best fit these skills.

MASTERED SKILLS

1.   6

2.   7.

3   8

4.   9
                                        .

5.   10

CAREER FIELDS OR POSITIONS THAT BEST UTILIZE THE ABOVE SKILLS

1.   6,

2.   7.

3.   8

4.   9

5.   10
.   .

Abstracting/Conceptualizing
  Parts of a system into a whole.
  Ideas for surface events.
  New spatial relationships.
Administering
  A department of people, programs.
  A specific activity, such as a test.
Advising
  Giving financial counsel, advice.
  Advice in an educational system.
Analyzing
  Quantitative data, statistical data.
  Human/social situations.
Anticipating
  Staying one step ahead of moods of the public.
  Being able to sense what will be fashionable in consumer goods.
  Expecting a problem before it develops, seeing first signs.
Appraising
  Evaluating programs or services.
  Judging the value of property.
  Evaluating performance of individuals.
Arranging
  Social functions, events.
  Meetings between specific people.
Assembling
  Technical apparatus or equipment.
  Items of information into a coherent whole.
Auditing
  Assessing the financial status of an organization.
Budgeting
  Outlining costs of a project.
  Assuring that money will not be spent in excess of funds. Using money efficiently and economically.
Calculating
  Performing mathematical computations.
  Assessing risks of an activity in advance.
Classifying
  Sorting information into categories.
Coaching
  Guiding activities of an athletic team.
  Tutoring in academic subjects or other pursuits on a one-to-one basis.
Collecting
  Money or services from people who owe.
  Widely scattered items.
  Many items in a single class (e. g. stamps).
Committee Working
  Attaining objectives through committee processes.
  Creating and implementing committee structures.
Compiling
  Gathering numerical, statistical data.
  Accumulating facts in a given topic area.
Computer Skills
  Keeping up with the latest software packages and new computers and all the bells and whistles

Interpreting
  Other languages.
  Obscure phrases or passages in English.
  Meaning of statistical data.
Interviewing
  Evaluating applicants to an organization.
  Obtaining information from others.
Investigating
  Seeking information which individuals may attempt to keep secret.
  Seeking the underlying causes of a problem.
Laboratory Working
  Setting up scientific equipment.
  Obtaining results from controlled experiments.
Listening
  To extended conversations between others.
  To extended conversation from one person.
  To recording devices or other listening situations
Locating
  Finding people who are missing
  Detecting missing information
  Sources of help for others
Making Layouts
  For printed media
  For public displays, posters
Managing
  Setting predetermined goals.
  Working ???
Mapping
  Mapping geographical, physical boundaries and space
  Putting sequences of events into graphic form
Measuring
  Obtaining accurate scientific measurements
Mediating
  Being a peacemaker between conflicting parties
  Acting as a liaison between competing interests or differing constituencies
Meeting the Public
  Being a receptionist or greeter
  Giving tours
  Being public representative of an agency
  Selling products in a public place
  Dealing with public in a service capacity (e. g., policeman or barber)
Moving with Dexterity
  Being able to move with speed and grace (sports, etc.)
Negotiating
  Financial contracts - Between individuals or groups in conflict

Confronting
Obtaining decisions from "reluctant dragons."
Giving bad news to others.
Obtaining information from others who are
unwilling to disclose it. Resolving personal
conflicts.

Initiating
Personal contacts with strangers.
New ideas, ways of doing things; new approaches.

Influencing others
Providing service to an individual
Serving a product such as food to individuals

Inspecting
Physical objects to meet standards.
People to determine criteria or detect information.

Outdoor Working
Involvement with the land and its resources
Involvement with animal life
Testing oneself against physical challenges
Involvement with wild animals
Collecting scientific data
Recasting land for commercial use

Persuading
Influencing others to see your point of view
Using influence with others when money is
Involved. Persuading others to help you

Planning
Anticipating future needs of a company or
organization
Scheduling a sequence of events
Arranging an itinerary for a trip

Politicking
Generating support for one's ideas within an
organization
Generating financial support from another agency
or organization

Predicting
Forecasting physical phenomena
Forecasting psychological asocial events
Forecasting the outcomes of contests
Forecasting economic trends

Preparing
Scientific equipment or specimens
Written materials for a presentation

Printing
Using mechanical printing equipment
Printing letters

Processing
The orderly flow of electronic data
Introducing an individual to procedures of an
organization
Identifying human interactions taking place in a
Group. Channeling information through a system

Programming
Electronic computers.
Developing and arranging sequence of events

Observing
Physical phenomena with accuracy - Behavior
of human beings social historical changes
Small details in physical objects - Small details
in written materials

Obtaining Information
From written sources, documents
From unwilling individuals

Operating
Scientific equipment
Mechanical devices, vehicles
Electronic data equipment, computers, etc.

Organizing
Bringing people together for certain tasks
Gathering information and arranging it in clear,
interpretable form
Arranging political activity; rousing the public
to action

Remembering
Large quantities of information for immediate
recall Names, faces, places, etc.
Long sequences of events or instructions

Repairing
Mechanical devices, equipment
Furniture, doors, walls, etc.

Repeating
Same procedure many times
Many attempts to obtain a difficult result

Representing
Representing an employer to the public

Researching
Extracting information from library, archives,
etc.
Obtaining information from other people
(surveys)
Obtaining information from physical data

Reviewing
Reassessing effects of a program
Assessing performance of an individual
Evaluating a play, movie, concert, recital, etc.

Rewriting
Technical language into popular form
Revising manuscripts

Selling
Ideas to others personally
Ideas through writing
Products to individuals
Policies to the public

Setting Up
Arranging for a demonstration of some physical
Apparatus. Getting people and things ready for
a show, an exhibit, etc.

Promoting
 Through written media
 On a personal basis, on-to-one
 Arranging financial backing
Proposal Writing
 For government funding
Protecting
 Protecting people from physical harm
 Protecting property from people
 Building protective devices or equipment
 Preventing destructive natural phenomena
Questioning
 Obtaining evidence in legal situations
 Asking creative questions in interview situations
Reading
 Reading large amounts of material quickly
 Reading written material with great care
 Reading numbers of symbols at a great distance
 Reading illegible or very small writing
Recording
 Numerical quantitative data
 Scientific data, using instruments
Record Keeping
 Orderly keeping of numerical data records
 Keeping log of sequential information
 Creating and maintaining files
 Clear and accurate financial records
 Record of services rendered
Recruiting/Staffing
 Attempting to acquire the services of people for an
 organization
Rehabilitating
 Helping people to resume use of limbs, etc., after
 Injury. Working with patients through non-physical
 media such as art, music, dance, etc.
Updating
 Keeping a file of information up-to-date
 Completing historical record of a person
 Acquiring new information on an old topic
Website Design
 Helping design a website
Working with Precision
 On physical materials
 With numerical data
 In time and space situation calling for little error
Writing
 Copywriting for sales
 Creative writing – prose, poetry
 Expository writing, essays
 Report of memo writing

Sketching
 Picture of things, people,
 Diagrams, Charts, other symbols
Speaking
 Speaking publicly to an audience
 Speaking individually to a group
 Speaking on electronic media (radio, TV, tape
recorder, etc.)
Supervising
 Directly supervising work of others in a white
collar setting
 Overseeing laborers
 Being responsible for maintenance of a physical
plant, building, set of apartments, etc.
Talking
 For long periods of time
 Able to sustain social chatter
Teaching
 In a school or college classroom
 Individuals to perform certain tasks
 Tutoring individuals in certain subjects
Team Unit Leader
 Working with a group
 Working with an individual
 Helping others be the best in their field
Timing
 Organizing time efficiently so that many tasks
 are completed
 in a finite time period
 Arranging an event so that it occurs at precisely
 the right
 moment
Tolerance
 Ability to accept misbehavior or mistakes by
people for
 whom you are responsible
 Being philosophical about lack of support for
work you are
 doing and misunderstanding; lack of reward or
 recognition
Translating
 Expressing words of one language in words of
 Another. Reducing sophisticated language to
 simpler terms
Treating
 Physical ailments of humans or animals
Trouble shooting
 Finding sources of difficulty in human relations
 Detecting sources of difficulty in physical
 apparatus

Task Six
Understand the World of Work-Review the 10 Groups of Industries Listed in the *Expanded Occupational Outlook Handbook*

Review positions in the <u>10 groups</u> that are in the 2010 *Enhanced Occupational Outlook Handbook*[13]

GROUP ONE- *MANAGEMENT, BUSINESS AND FINANCIAL OPERATION OCCUPATIONS*
Business and Financial Operations Occupations
>Accountants and Auditors
>Appraisers and Assessors of Real Estate
>Budget Analysts
>Claims Adjusters, Appraisers, Examiners, and Investigators
>Cost Estimators
>Financial Analysts and personal Financial Advisors
>Insurance Underwriters
>Loan Officers
>Management Analysts
>Meeting and Convention Planners
>Tax Examiners, Collectors, and Revenue Agents

Management Occupations
>Administrative Services Managers
>Advertising, Marketing, Promotions, Public relations, and Sales Managers
>Computer and Information Systems Managers
>Construction Managers
>Education Administrators
>Engineering and Natural Sciences Managers
>Farmers, Ranchers, and Agricultural Managers
>Financial Managers
>Food Service Managers
>Funeral Directors
>Human Resources, Training, and Labor Relations Managers and Specialists
>Industrial Production Managers
>Lodging Managers
>Medical and health Services Managers
>Property, Real Estate, and Community
>Association Managers
>Purchasing Managers, Buyers, and Purchasing Agents
>Top Executives

GROUP TWO-PROFESSIONAL AND RELATED OCCUPATIONS

Architects, Surveyors, and Cartographers
Architects, Except Landscape and Naval
Landscape Architects
Surveyors, Cartographers, Photogrammetrists and Mapping Technicians

Art and Design Occupations
Artists and Related Workers
Commercial and Industrial Designers
Fashion Designers
Floral Designers
Graphic Designers
Interior Designers

Community and Social Services Occupations
Counselors
Health Educators
Probation Officers and Correctional Treatment Specialists
Social and Human Service Assistants, Social Workers

Computer and Mathematical Occupations
Actuaries
Computer Programmers
Computer Scientists and Database Administrators
Computer Software Engineers
Computer Support Specialists and Systems Administrators
Computer Systems Analysts
Mathematicians
Operations Research Analysts
Statisticians

Drafters and Engineering Technicians
Drafters
Engineering Technicians

Education, Training, Library, and Museum Occupations
Archivists, Curators, and Museum Technicians
Instructional Coordinators
Librarians
Library Technicians
Teacher Assistants
Teachers – Adult Literacy and Remedial Education
Teachers – Postsecondary
Teachers – Preschool, Kindergarten, Elementary, Middle, and Secondary
Teachers – Self-Enrichment Education
Teachers – Special Education

Entertainers and Performers, Sports and Related Occupations
Actors, Producers, and Directors
Athletes, Coaches, Umpires and Related Workers
Dancers and Choreographers
Musicians, Singers, and Related Workers

Health Diagnosing and Treating Occupations

Audiologists
Chiropractors
Dentists
Dietitians and Nutritionists
Occupational Therapists
Optometrists
Pharmacists
Physical Therapists
Physician Assistants
Physicians and Surgeons
Podiatrists
Radiation Therapists Recreational Therapists
Registered Nurses
Respiratory Therapists
Speech-Language Pathologists
Veterinarians

Health Technologists and Technicians

Athletic Trainers
Cardiovascular Technologists and Technicians
Clinical Laboratory Technologists and Technicians
Dental Hygienists
Diagnostic Medical Sonographers
Emergency Medical Technicians and Paramedics
Licensed Practical and Licensed Vocational Nurses
Medical Records and health Information technicians
Nuclear Medicine Technologists
Occupational Health and Safety Specialists and Technicians
Opticians, Dispensing
Pharmacy Technicians
Radiologic Technologists and Technicians
Surgical Technologists
Veterinary Technologists and Technicians

Legal Occupations

Court Reporters, Paralegals and legal Assistants
Judges, Magistrates, and Other Judicial Workers
Lawyers

Life Scientists

Agricultural and Food Scientists
Biological Scientists
Conservation Scientists and Forester, Medical Scientists

Media and Communications-Related Occupations
     Announcers
     Broadcast and Sound Engineering Technicians and Radio Operators
     Interpreters and Translators
     News Analysts, Reporters and Correspondents
     Photographers
     Public Relations Specialists
     Television, Video and Motion Picture Camera Operators and Editors
     Writers and Editors

Physical Scientists
     Atmospheric Scientists
     Chemists and Material Scientists
     Environmental Scientists and hydrologists
     Geoscientists
     Physicists and Astronomers

Social Scientists and Related Occupations
     Economists
     Market and Survey Researchers
     Psychologists
     Urban and Regional Planners
     Social Scientists, Other
     Science Technicians

GROUP THREE- SERVICE OCCUPATIONS
Building and Grounds Cleaning and Maintenance Occupations
     Building Cleaning Workers
     Grounds Maintenance Workers
     Pest Control Workers

Food Preparation and Serving Related Occupations
     Chefs, Cooks, and Food Preparation Workers
     Food and Beverage Serving and Related Workers

Healthcare Support Occupations
     Dental Assistants
     Massage Therapists
     Medical Assistants
     Medical Transcriptionists
     Nursing, Psychiatric, and Home Health Aides
     Occupational Therapist Assistants and Aides
     Pharmacy Aides
     Physical Therapists Assistants and Aides

Personal Care and Service Occupations
       Animal Care and Service Workers
       Barbers, Cosmetologists, and Other Personal Appearance Workers
       Child Care Workers
       Fitness Workers
       Flight Attendants
       Gaming Services Occupations
       Personal and Home Care Aides
       Recreation Workers

Protective Service Occupations
       Correctional Officers
       Fire Fighting Occupations
       Police and Detectives

GROUP FOUR- SALES AND RELATED OCCUPATIONS
       Advertising Sales Agents
       Cashiers
       Counter and Rental Clerks
       Demonstrators, Product Promoters, and Models
       Insurance Sales Agents
       Real Estate Brokers and Sales Agents
       Retail Salespersons
       Sales Engineers
       Sales Representatives, Wholesale and Manufacturing
       Sales Worker Supervisors
       Securities, Commodities, and Financial Services Sales Agents
       Travel Agents

GROUP FIVE- OFFICE AND ADMINISTRATIVE SUPPORT OCCUPATIONS

Financial Clerks
       Bill and Account Collectors
       Billing and Posting Clerks and Machine Operators
       Bookkeeping, Accounting, and Auditing Clerks
       Gamming Cage Workers
       Payroll and Timekeeping Clerks
       Procurement Clerks
       Tellers

Information and Record Clerks
Brokerage Clerks
Credit Authorizers, Checkers, and Clerks
Customer Service Representatives
File Clerks

Hotel, Motel, and Resort Desk Clerks
Human Resources Assistants, Except Payroll and Timekeeping
Interviewers
Library Assistants, Clerical
Receptionists and Information Clerks
Reservation and Transportation Ticket Agents and Travel Clerks

Material Recording, Scheduling, Dispatching, and Distributing Occupations
Cargo and Freight Agents
Couriers and Messengers
Dispatchers
Meter Readers, Utilities
Postal Service Workers
Production, Planning, and Expediting Clerks
Shipping, Receiving, and Traffic Clerks
Stock Clerks and Order Fillers
Weighers, Measurers, Checkers, and Samplers, Recordkeeping

Other Office and Administrative Support Occupations
Communications Equipment Operators
Computer Operators
Data Entry and Information Processing Workers
Desktop Publishers
Office and Administrative Support Worker Supervisors and Managers
Office Clerks, General
Secretaries and Administrative Assistants

GROUP SIX- FARMING, FISHING, AND FORESTRY OCCUPATIONS
Agricultural Workers
Fishers and Fishing Vessel Operators
Forest, Conservation, and Logging Workers

GROUP SEVEN- CONSTRUCTION TRADES AND RELATED WORKERS
Boilermakers
Brickmasons, Blockmasons, and Stonemasons
Carpenters
Carpet, Floor, and Tile Installers and Finishers
Cement Masons, Concrete Finishers, Segmental Pavers and Terrazzo
Workers

Construction and Building Inspectors
Construction Equipment Operators
Construction Laborers
Drywall Installers, Ceiling Tile Installers, and Tapers
Electricians
Elevator Installers and Repairers
Glaziers
Hazardous Materials Removal Workers
Insulation Workers
Painters and paperhangers
Pipelayers, Plumbers, Pipefitters, and Steamfitters
Plasterers and Stucco Masons
Roofers
Sheet Metal Workers
Structural and Reinforcing Iron and Metal Workers

GROUP EIGHT- INSTALLATION, MAINTENANCE, AND REPAIR OCCUPATIONS
Electrical and Electronic Equipment Mechanics, Installers, and Repairers
Computer, Automated Teller, and Office Machine Repairers
Electrical and Electronics Installers and Repairers
Electronic Home Entertainment Equipment Installers and Repairers
Radio and Telecommunications Equipment Installers and Repairers

Other Installation, Maintenance, and Repair Occupations
Coin, Vending, and Amusement Machine Servicers and Repairers
Heating, air-Conditioning, and Refrigeration Mechanics and Installers
Home Appliance Repairers
Industrial Machinery Mechanics and Maintenance Workers
Line Installers and Repairers
Maintenance and Repair Workers, General
Millwrights
Precision Instrument and Equipment Repairers

Vehicle and Mobile Equipment Mechanics, Installers, and Repairers
Aircraft and Avionics Equipment Mechanics and Service Technicians
Automotive Body and Related Repairers
Automotive Service Technicians and Mechanics
Heavy Vehicle and Mobile Equipment Service Technicians and Mechanics
Small Engine Mechanics

GROUP NINE – *PRODUCTION OCCUPATIONS*
Assemblers and Fabricators
Food Processing Occupations

Metal Workers and Plastic Workers
Computer Control Programmers and Operators
Machine Setters, Operators, and Tenders-Metal and Plastic
Machinists
Tool and Die Makers
Welding, Soldering, and Brazing Workers

Other Production Occupations
Inspectors, testers, Sorters, Samplers, and Weighers
Jewelers and Precious Stone and Metal workers
Medical, Dental, and Ophthalmic Laboratory Technicians
Painting and Coating Workers, Except Construction and Maintenance
Photographic Process Workers and Processing Machine Operators
Semiconductor Processors

Plant and System Operators
Power Plant Operators, Distributors, and Dispatchers
Stationary Engineers and Boiler Operators
Water and Liquid Waste Treatment Plant and System Operators

Printing Occupations
Bookbinders and Bindery Workers
Prepress Technicians and Workers
Printing Machine Operators
Textile, Apparel, and Furnishings Occupations
Woodworkers

GROUP 10-*TRANSPORTATION AND MATERIAL MOVING OCCUPATIONS*
Air Transportation Occupations-
Air Traffic Controllers
Aircraft Pilots
Flight Engineers
Material Moving Occupations-Truck Drivers
Motor Vehicle Operators-Bus Drivers, Taxi Drivers and Chauffeurs,
Truck Drivers
Rail Transportation Occupations
Water Transportation Occupations

There are many college graduates who have done internships and worked in the trade and construction business to learn the ropes and then they started their own company becoming the owner and CEO. They applied what they learned in their business and management courses in college to what they learned about the trade. Which career areas appeal to you?

Task Seven-
Understand the World of Work-Review the 115 Top Projected Career Positions until 2015 and Select Several That Appeal to You

The following 115 career positions are the highest growing jobs in America as projected by the US Department of Labor and US Bureau of Labor Statistics[14]. We will position them based on percentage growth over the next decade. Careers should match your interests, personality, and capability. If you are interested in a particular position, Google it by name to learn more about the position. You can also conduct information interviews with people in these positions. Which of these areas fall in your high career interest areas on the ACT test?

40 percent plus growth positions

1. medical assistants	52% growth
2. physician assistants	50% growth
3. computer software engineers	46% growth
4. dental hygienists	43% growth
5. dental assistants	43% growth
6. computer scientists and database administrators	40% growth
7. physical therapist assistants	40% growth

30 to 39 percent growth position

8. physical therapists	37% growth
9. veterinary technologists	35% growth
10. diagnostic medical sonographers	35% growth
11. medical scientists	34% growth
12. occupational therapists	34% growth
13. cardiovascular technologists and technicians	33% growth
14. occupational therapist assistants	33% growth
15. teachers – post secondary	32% growth
16. nursing, psychiatric and home health aids	32% growth
17. computer system analysts	31% growth
18. hazard materials removal workers	31% growth
19. paralegals and legal assistants	30% growth
20. social and human service assistants	30% growth
21. surgical technologists	30% growth

20 to 29 percent growth positions

22. athletic trainers	29% growth
23. medical records and health information assistants	29% growth
24. pharmacy technicians	29% growth
25. registered nurses	29% growth
26. computer support specialists	28% growth
27. instructional coordinators in schools	28% growth
28. fitness workers	27% growth
29. emergency medical technicians and paramedics	27% growth
30. computer and information system managers	26% growth
31. radiation therapists	26% growth

32. pharmacists	25% growth
33. teachers – self-enrichment education	25% growth
34. taxi drivers and chauffeurs	25% growth
35. physicians and surgeons	24% growth
36. massage therapists	24% growth
37. animal care and service workers	24% growth
38. gaming service occupations	24% growth
39. medical transciptionists	23% growth
40. fire fighting occupations	23% growth
41. counter and retail clerks	23% growth
42. public relations specialists	23% growth
43. respiratory therapists	23% growth
44. clinical laboratory technologists	23% growth
45. medical and health service managers	23% growth
46. appraisers and assessors of real estate	23% growth
47. actuaries	23% growth
48. human resources, training and labor relations mgrs.	23% growth
49. desktop publishers	23% growth
50. customer service representatives	23% growth
51. meeting and convention planners	22% growth
52. social workers	22% growth
53. receptionists and information clerks	22% growth
54. construction and building inspectors	22% growth
55. chiropractors	22% growth
56. accountants and auditors	22% growth
57. financial analysts and personal financial advisors	21% growth
58. nuclear medicine technologists	21% growth
59. bill and account collectors	21% growth
60. teachers – special education	21% growth
61. counselors	21% growth
62. advertising, marketing, promotions, PR and sales	20% growth
63. management analysts	20% growth
64. market and survey researchers	20% growth
65. interpreters and translators	20% growth
66. athletes, coaches, umpires and related workers	20% growth
67. optometrists	20% growth

15 to 19 percent growth

68. environmental scientists and hydrologists	19% growth
69. psychologists	19% growth
70. landscape architects	19% growth
71. ground maintenance workers	19% growth
72. private detectives and investigators	18% growth
73. cost estimators	18% growth
74. dietitians and nutritionists	18% growth

75. pest control workers	18% growth
76. teachers – pre-school, kindergarten, elementary	18% growth
77. administrative service managers	17% growth
78. education administrators	17% growth
79. lodging managers	17% growth
80. veterinarians	17% growth
81. writers and editors	17% growth
82. top executives	17% growth
83. architects, except landscape and naval	17% growth
84. biological scientists	17% growth
85. atmospheric scientists	17% growth
86. licensed, practical and vocational nurses	17% growth
87. dancers and choreographers	17% growth
88. recreational workers	17% growth
89. retail sales persons	17% growth
90. interior designers	16% growth
91. actors, producers and directors	16% growth
92. teachers – adult literacy and remedial education	16% growth
93. barbers, cosmetologists, appearance workers	16% growth
94. flight attendants	16% growth
95. advertising sales agents	16% growth
96. food and beverage serving and related workers	16% growth
97. podiatrists	16% growth
98. police and detectives	16% growth
99. TV, video and motion picture operators, editors	16% growth
100. speech – language pathologists	15% growth
101. financial managers	15% growth
102. property, real estate, association managers	15% growth
103. court reporters	15% growth
104. lawyers	15% growth
105. graphic designers	15% growth
106. archivists, curators and museum technicians	15% growth
107. broadcast and sound engineering technicians	15% growth
108. chefs, cooks and food preparation workers	15% growth
109. childcare workers	15% growth
110. urban and regional planners	15% growth
111. claims adjustors, appraisers and examiners	15% growth
112. sales representatives, wholesale and manufacturing	15% growth
113. automotive service technicians	15% growth
114. securities, commodities and financial agents	15% growth
115. nannies or live-in child care takers	15% growth

Task Eight-
Understand the World of Work- Review the Majors Offered by Colleges and Universities and Select Several That Appeal to You.

You should review the following majors and identify those majors that might be a good fit in relation to academic strengths and career interests on the ACT test[15]. Go to google and type in major and ask for related occupations.

AGRICULTURE & AGRICULTURAL TECH.
Agricultural Business
Agricultural Economics
Agricultural Mechanics
Agricultural Production/Technology
Agronomy (e.g., field crop management, soils)
Animal Sciences (e.g., animal breeding, dairy, poultry)
Farm and Ranch Management
Fish, Game and Wildlife Management
Food Sciences/Technology
Forestry (pre-forestry) and related Sciences
Horticulture/Ornamental Horticulture
Natural Resources (air, water, soil, etc.) Management

ARCHITECTURE & ENVIRONMENTAL DESIGN
Architectural Drafting
Architecture (pre-architecture)
Building Construction/Construction Science
City, Community, and Regional Planning
Environmental Design
Interior Design
Landscape Architecture

BUSINESS & MANAGEMENT
Accounting
Banking and Finance
Business Administration and Management
Business Economics
Contract Management & Procurement/Purchasing
Hotel/Motel/Restaurant Management
Human Resources Development/Training
Institutional Management
Insurance and Risk Management

International Business/Management
Labor/Industrial Relations
Management Information Systems
Management Science
Marketing Management and Research
Organizational Behavior
Personnel Management
Real Estate
Small Business Management/Ownership
Trade and Industrial Supervision and Management
Transportation Management

BUSINESS & OFFICE
Bookkeeping
Business Data Processing/Computer Operation
Court Reporting
Office Supervision and Management
Secretarial (including executive, legal, medical)
Typing and General Office
Word Processing

MARKETING & DISTRIBUTION
Fashion Merchandising
Retailing and Sales
Travel Services and Tourism

COMMUNICATION & COMMUNICATIONS TECH.
Advertising
Commercial Art
Graphic and Printing Communications
Journalism
Photographic/Motion Picture Technology
Public Relations
Radio/Television Broadcasting
Radio/Television Production and Technology

COMMUNITY & PERSONAL SERVICES

Corrections
Cosmetology/Barbering
Criminal Justice/Criminology
Fire Protection/Fire Control & Safety
 Technology
Funeral Services/Mortuary Science
Law Enforcement and Administration
Library Science/Library Assisting
Military Science/Technology
Parks and Recreation
Public Administration
Public Affairs
Social Work

COMPUTER & INFORMATION SCIENCES

Computer Programming
Computer Science
Data Processing Information Sciences and
Systems
Math/computer Science

CROSS-DISCIPLINARY STUDIES

Area and Ethnic Studies (e.g., Latin
American studies, African American
studies)
Liberal General Studies
Multi-Interdisciplinary Studies (e.g., peace
studies, women's studies

EDUCATION

Adult and Continuing Education
Education Administration
Elementary Education
Junior High/Middle School Education
Pre-elementary (early childhood) Education
Secondary Education
Student Counseling
Teacher Aide

TEACHER EDUCATION

Agricultural Education
Art Education
Business Education
English Education
Foreign Languages Education
Health Education

Home Economics Family & Consumer
Services Education
Industrial Arts Education
Mathematics Education
Music Education
Physical Education
Science Education
Social Studies/Social Sciences Education
Special Education (e.g., learning disabled,
gifted)
Speech Correction Education
Teaching English as a Second Language
Technical/Trade and Industrial Education
Education, Other Subject Area

ENGINEERING (PRE-ENGINEERING)

Aerospace, Aeronautical & Astronautical
Engineering
Agricultural Engineering
Architectural Engineering
Bioengineering and Biomedical Engineering
Ceramic Engineering
Chemical Engineering
Civil Engineering
Computer Engineering
Construction Engineering/Construction
Management
Electrical, Electronics, & Communications
Engineering
Engineering Management
Engineering Physics
Engineering Science
Environmental Health Engineering
Geological and Geophysical Engineering
Industrial Engineering
Materials Engineering
Mechanical Engineering
Mining and Mineral Engineering
Naval Architecture and Marine Engineering
Nuclear Engineering
Ocean Engineering
Petroleum Engineering
Systems Engineering

ENGINEERING-RELATED TECHNOLOGIES

Aeronautical Technology
Air Conditioning, Heating & Refrigeration Technology
Architectural Design
Biomedical Equipment Technology
Civil Technology
Computer Technology
Construction Technology
Drafting and Design Technology
Electrical Technology
Electronic Technology
Electromechanical Instrumentation & Maintenance Technology
Environmental Control Technology
Industrial Production Technology
Laser Electro-Optic Technology
Manufacturing Technology
Mechanical Design Technology
Mining and Petroleum Technology
Occupational Safety & Health Technology
Surveying and Mapping Technology
Engineering-Related Technologies, Other

FOREIGN LANGUAGES

Asiatic languages (eg. Chinese, Japanese, Korean)
Classical Languages (e.g., Greek, Latin)
French
German
Italian
Middle Eastern Languages (e.g., Arabic, Hebrew)
Russian
Spanish
Foreign languages, Other

HEALTH SCIENCES & ALLIED HEALTH FIELDS

Chiropractic (pre-chiropractic)
Dental Assisting
Dental Hygiene
Dental Laboratory/Technology
Dentistry (pre-dentistry)
Emergency Medical Technology-Ambulance/Paramedic

Health Care Administration
Medical/Surgical Assisting
Medical Laboratory/technology
Medical Records Administration/Technology
Medicine (pre-medicine)
Mental Health & Human Services/Technology
Nuclear Medical Technology
Nursing (practical nursing)
Nursing (registered/BSN)
Occupational Therapy/Assisting
Optometry (pre-optometry)
Pharmacy (pre-pharmacy)
Physician Assisting
Physical Therapy/Assisting
Radiology/Radiologic Technology
Recreational/Art/Music Therapy
Respiratory Therapy/Technology
Speech Pathology/Audiology
Veterinarian Assisting
Veterinary Medicine (pre-veterinary medicine)

HOME ECONOMICS/FAMILY & CONSUMER SERVICES

Child Development, Care, and Guidance
Child Care Aide/Assisting
Culinary Arts (chef/cook)
Family/Consumer Resource Management
Fashion Design
Food Production, Management, and Services
Food Sciences & Human Nutrition/Dietetics
Human Environment and Housing
Individual and family Development
Textiles and Clothing

LETTERS

Classics
Comparative Literature
Creative Writing
English, general
Linguistics
Literature, English/American
Speech, Debate and Forensics

MATHEMATICS
Actuarial Sciences
Applied Mathematics
Statistics
PHILOSOPHY, RELIGION, & THEOLOGY
Bible Studies
Philosophy
Religion
Religious Education
Religious Music
Theology
SCIENCES (BIOLOGICAL & PHYSICAL)
Astronomy
Atmospheric Sciences and meteorology
Biochemistry and Biophysics
Biology
Botany
Chemistry
Earth Science
Ecology
Geology
Microbiology
Oceanography
Physics
Zoology
SOCIAL SCIENCES
Anthropology
Economics Geography
History International Relations
Law (pre-law)
Paralegal/Legal Assisting
Political Science/Government
Psychology

Sociology
Urban Studies
TRADE & INDUSTRIAL
Aircraft Mechanics
Airplane Piloting and navigation
Automotive Body Repair
Automotive Mechanics and Technology
Aviation Management
Computer Electronics/Repair
Construction Trades and Carpentry
Diesel Engine Mechanics and Technology
Drafting
Electrical & Electronics Equipment Repair
Heating, Air Conditioning & Refrigeration Mechanics
Machine Tool Operation/machine Shop
Mechanical Drafting
Welding and Welding Technology
VISUAL & PERFORMING ARTS
Applied Design/Crafts (e.g., ceramics, glass, jewelry, weaving)
Art (e.g., painting, drawing, sculpture)
Art History and Appreciation
Cinematography/Film/Video
Dance
Design, General
Dramatic Arts
Fine Arts, General
Graphic Arts Technology
Graphic Design
Music (liberal arts)
Music Performance
Music Theory and Composition
Photography

Task Nine-
Understand the World of Work
Learn How to Conduct an Exploratory or Informational Interview to Gain Information on Organizations and Industries.©

If you are not certain about your future career, it is recommended that you use your contacts and the informational interview to learn about industries, companies and functional areas (positions) that would be the fit for you. This requires you identifying people from different industries and functional areas and contacting them to set up an appointment.

The informational/exploratory interview allows you to both learn and sell yourself to a targeted employer without the stress typically associated with the hiring process. Your main goal is not to elicit a job offer now, but to make a positive impression and acquire enough information about the industry and functional areas to know this is place where you want to work to start your career.

The informational interview has several secondary goals. First, it allows you to gain valuable-confidence in the interview situation, while meeting face-to-face with potential employers. The informational interview is a low-stress interview that permits you to gain confidence with new jargon, and may open the door to referrals and/or additional contacts. Secondly, it is possible that this interview could, in fact, lead to a job offer. At the very least, it will help you identify the person who has the power to hire you.

Arranging an Informational/Low Stress Interview

1. Make personal contact.
2. Indicate referral source.
3. State purpose of call.
4. Arrange interview.

The most effective method for arranging a low-stress interview is through a personal contact, either by phone or in person.

(Phone) " ___(Mr., Mrs., Miss, Ms.), _____ it's Sally Atwood calling."
(In person) "(Mr., Mrs., Miss, Ms.), _____ , hi! I'm Sally Atwood."

Next, indicate the referral source or how you know the person.

Examples: "I go to school with your daughter Cassandra."
"My friend John Davis recommended that I speak with you.

State the purpose of your call.
Examples: "I am graduating next year and attempting to gain information about different industries starting with yours.

(If you know the industry):
"I am seeking a career in the _____ industry and I was hoping you could provide me with information about the future of your industry as you see it, and how you would recommend someone like me enter your industry."

116

(If you know someone in your targeted position):

"I am seeking an entry-level sales position, but before beginning to actively market myself, I wanted to explore the job with someone who has experience in sales. You were recommended as someone who could give me information about this career position."

Arrange the interview.

Examples: "The next time you are on campus to visit Cassandra, could we get together for 10 or 15 minutes?"
"Would it be possible to take you to lunch one day?"
"Could we set up a time where I could call on you for some information?"

Preparing for the Informational/Low-Stress Interview

Before the interview, study the information you accumulated about the person's company, the industry, or the person you'll be talking to. Think about questions to ask. It always helps to appear knowledgeable about the subject, to show that your interest is genuine. Jot down the questions you'll ask. Be prepared to take notes during the interview; not to do so would defeat the whole purpose of the interview and that is to gather information.

Remember to listen carefully. Everything you learn during this interview is of potential use to you later. Also, the more professional you appear and behave, the more positive view the person will have of you.. By the way, be sure to bring a copy of your resume, just in case!

Conducting the Informational/Low-Stress Interview

It is usually best to start with a non-threatening personal question such as, "How did you begin to work in this industry?" and "How long have you been in this field?"

The following list of questions is designed to give you some suggestions and also to indicate the importance of preparation before conducting a informational/low-stress interview.

1. How would you classify the industry in which you work?
2. How long have you been in this industry?
3. What were you doing prior to entering this industry?
4. Why did you choose this particular industry?
5. How did you happen to join this particular company?
6. What was your first position and what steps did you take to get where you are today?
6. What is the next step up the ladder for you, in terms of position and/or areas of interest?
7. Where could you see yourself in five or ten years from now, in this particular field?
8. How does one know what position he/she best fits?
9. What special training/skills must an individual possess to do your job?
10. What courses would you recommend that I take that could give me a head start??
11. What is a good major to take for someone who wants to do the job you are doing or to enter this industry?

12. when you interview a new college graduate, what are some of the questions you would ask the student? What would you be looking for in a new employee?
13. Where do most young people interviewing for a job shoot themselves in the foot?
14. What are typical starting incomes in your field/industry for an entry level position and how do the salaries escalate by various levels? What would be the leveling-off point?
15. Would you classify your company as a main-line company in this industry, or would it be classed as an ancillary, or feeder, company to the main-line?
16. If this is a main-line company, what segment of the industry do you fill?
17. If this company is a feeder industry, what segment of the main-line industry do you fill?
18. How big is your industry in terms of dollar production and volume?
19. What has its growth been over the past five years? Ten years? Fifteen years?
20. What does the future hold for your 'industry in five years? Ten years? Fifteen years?
21. Who would you classify as your major competitors? How do you rank in relation to them? In other words, what makes your product or service better to these competitors, and why?
22. What does the future hold in relation to this competitive edge?
23. How many positions or departments would an average-size company in your field have? What would these be (i.e., purchasing, manufacturing, sales, marketing)?
24. Could you give me a brief description of the function of the various divisions of the organization?
25. How are the individuals trained in these various areas? Is the training through practical application or is it just picked up on a day-to-day basis through job performance?
26. Is your industry unionized, or is there a common association throughout?
27. What would constitute a good increase in overall production or service: dollar volume of sales, gross manufactured product, employee retention?
28. Is your industry or service seasonal? If so, to what extent?
29. What type of employee incentives are offered throughout the industry?
30. What type of benefit plans are available to people in a company like yours and/or throughout the industry?
31. Is there much attrition in your field as far as staff or personnel are concerned?
32. What would be the main contributing factor; do you feel, in the turnover of people in your industry?
33. What would you say is the single most important (strength, product, service) your industry offers?
34. If you were an employer, what would you look for in an employee, from an entry-level position on up through a position like yours?

Try to end the interview by obtaining a lead or a second contact. You can often do this by asking a question such as, "Could you give me the name of the individual in your company that is in charge of sales and marketing. I would like to learn more about this area since I am leaning toward going into sales and marketing. " You might also consider ending the interview by saying "I've brought a copy of my resume; would you be willing to take a look at it?"

Always thank the person for giving you the time and their attention. You should contact the person three or four months before graduating and see if he/she can help you get in front of the person who hires sales people in their company. You should also tell the person when and where you landed a job. People appreciate you telling them. They can also help you in the future.

Task Ten
Understand the World of Work:
Learn About Job Opportunities for College Graduates

Wondering where the jobs will be in the future? Government economists estimated which occupations will grow fastest between 2002 and 2014. They also predicted which occupations would have the most new jobs.

Career Opportunities for College Students

- *10 Fastest Growing Occupations for College Graduates*

- *Occupations with the Most New Jobs: Associate's Degrees or Postsecondary Vocational Awards*

- *Occupations with the Most New Jobs: Bachelor's Degrees*

10 Fastest Growing Occupations for College Grads

Occupation	2002	2014	Percent Change
Network systems and data communications analysts	186,000	292,000	57%
Physician assistants	63,000	94,000	49%
Medical records and health information technicians	147,000	216,000	47%
Computer software engineers, applications	394,000	573,000	46%
Computer software engineers, systems software	281,000	409,000	46%
Physical therapist assistants	50,000	73,000	46%
Fitness trainers and aerobics instructors	183,000	264,000	45%
Database administrators	110,000	159,000	44%
Veterinary technologists and technicians	53,000	76,000	44%
Dental hygienists	148,000	212,000	43%

Occupations with the Most New Jobs: Associate's Degrees

SOURCE: United States Bureau of Labor Statistics

Occupation	2002	2014	Change
Registered nurses	2,284,000	2,908,000	623%
Computer support specialists	507,000	660,000	153%
Preschool teachers, except special education	424,000	577,000	153%
Licensed practical and licensed vocational nurses	702,000	844,000	142%
Automotive service technicians and mechanics	818,000	919,000	101%
Hairdressers, hairstylists, and cosmetologists	585,000	671,000	86%
Fitness trainers and aerobics instructors	183,000	264,000	81%
Medical records and health information technicians	147,000	216,000	69%
Dental hygienists	148,000	212,000	64%
Emergency medical technicians and paramedics	179,000	238,000	59%

Occupations with the Most New Jobs: Bachelor's Degrees

Occupation	2002	2014	Change
Elementary school teachers, except special education	1,467,000	1,690,000	223%
Accountants and auditors	1,055,000	1,261,000	205%
Computer systems analysts	468,000	653,000	184%
Secondary school teachers, except special and vocational education	988,000	1,167,000	180%
Computer software engineers, applications	394,000	573,000	179%
Special education teachers	433,000	563,000	130%
Computer software engineers, systems software	281,000	409,000	128%
Network systems and data communications analysts	186,000	292,000	106%
Network and computer systems administrators	251,000	345,000	94%
Computer programmers	499,000	571,000	73%

Ten Industries with the Fastest Employment Growth

Wondering which industries will provide the jobs of the future? Government economists estimated which industries would grow fastest between 2002 and 2014.

Industry	2002	2014	Percent Change
Software publishers	256,000	430,000	68%
Management, scientific, and technical consulting services	732,000	1,137,000	55%
Community care facilities for the elderly and residential care facilities not classified elsewhere	695,000	1,078,000	55%
Computer systems design and related services	1,163,000	1,798,000	55%
Employment services	3,249,000	5,012,000	54%
Individual, family, community, and vocational rehabilitation services	1,269,000	1,867,000	47%
Ambulatory health care services except offices of health practitioners	1,444,000	2,113,000	46%
Internet services, data processing, and other information services	529,000	773,000	46%
Water, sewage, and other systems	49,000	71,000	45%
Child day care services	734,000	1,050,000	43%

SOURCE: United States Bureau of Labor Statistics

Which positions appeal to you the most?

Franchise Organizations-Review Appendix C which lists the 105 Fastest Growing Franchises in America. List below a few that appeal to you the most? Could you work in the one you like the most to gain experience and then buy a franchise later?

Task 11
Create a Career Profile from the Information Accumulated and Select a Tentative Career Field/Path and Major to Pursue
Copyright © 2012 Michael V. Mulligan

MY CAREER PROFILE

PROFESSIONAL EDUCATIONAL AND PROFESSIONAL CREDENTIALS

HIGH SCHOOL:	FR	SOPH	JR	SR
COLLEGE:	FR	SOPH	JR	SR
VOCATIONAL SCHOOL:	CERTIFICATION:			
GRADUATE SCHOOL:	DEGREE RECEIVED:			

	HIGH SCHOOL	**COLLEGE**	**COLLEGE**
NAME OF SCHOOL AND LOCATION:			
DATES OF ATTENDANCE:			
APPROXIMATE G.P.A. OR CLASS STANDING:			
COLLEGE MAJOR/MINOR STUDIES			
FAVORITE SUBJECT(S):			
OFFICES HELD, HONORS, AWARDS:			
EXTRA-CURRICULAR ACTIVITIES:			

PROFESSIONAL CERTIFICATES ACQUIRED.

REVIEW YOUR PAST CAREER PATH

PLEASE LIST THE COMPANIES/ORGANIZATIONS THAT HIRED YOU, THEIR INDUSTRY, THE DATES OR TIME LINE YOU WORKED THERE AND THE POSITIONS/JOBS THAT YOU HELD.

#	COMPANIES OR ORGANIZATIONS	INDUSTRY	DATES EMPLOYED	POSITIONS/INTERNSHIPS HELD
1				
2				
3				
4				
5				
6				

WHAT CAREER FIELD OR POSITION(S) HAVE THESE WORK EXPERIENCES PREPARED YOU TO DO NEXT?

_____

_____

_____

Review the Information Gathered from Tasks Three through 10 in Goal Four

Task Three-What did you write down as your career aspiration and why?

Task Four- How did you rank the *four work tasks* and which of the career areas under your top *work task* did you show the most interest?

Task Five- Which *10 Skills* have you mastered and which career areas do they best fit under?

Task Six-Which three *Groups of Industries* of the 10 did you rank the highest in regard to your interests and why?

Task Seven- Of the 115 top projected career positions, which 10 appealed to you the most and why?

Task Eight- When you reviewed the many college majors listed, which five appealed to you the most and why?

Task Nine- In which industries and companies do you want to set up and conduct an exploratory and informational interview?

Task 10- Which career opportunities for college graduates appealed to you the most? Would you want to buy and operate a franchise some day? Which franchise?

Develop and Execute a Plan so You Obtain a Good Job
Just Before or Right After Graduation

Page

127 **Task One** – Identify a Tentative Career Field/Path and Major and
Take the Courses that Will Help You Land a Good Job

133 **Task Two**- Know the Challenges Facing You after Graduation
so You Can Use Your College Education to Prepare for Them

135 **Task Three** – Develop a Plan on What You are Going to Do During
The College Years to Build You a Resume That Will Land You a Job
at Graduation

136 **Task Four** – Develop a Job Search Plan and Implement It Your
Freshman Year so You Obtain Interviews and a Good Job Offer
at Graduation

148 **Task Five**– Identify the Work Factors that You Want in the Position
You are Pursuing.

149 **Task Six**- Prepare Yourself for Interviews and How to Negotiate so
You Obtain Job Offers Just Before or Right After Graduation

155 **Task Seven**-Review what the Professionals Say about Advancing
Your Career

159 **Appendix A**- Sample Resumes

185 **Appendix B**- Sample Letters

202 **Appendix C**-105 Fastest Growing Franchises in America

Task One
Select a Tentative Career Field/Path and Major and
Take the Courses that Will Help You Land a Good Job
At Graduation and Launch Your Career Journey

As soon as you can identify a career field to enter or career path to follow, the more it will help you select a major and courses that can help you obtain a job in your chosen career field and launch your career journey. However, there are three points you need to remember. The first is that you go to college to broaden your knowledge, learn how to think and take courses that could help you move into a special career field and position.. This position might require an A.A or B.A. or B.S. degree. The second is if you are a fairly good student, you will probably want to go to graduate or professional school and prepare yourself for a special career. The third point is you will meet a number of people in the work place who can help you launch your career. You do not know how much you will grow, who you will meet and what opportunities might lie ahead. This is why it is impossible to predict where we will be 10, 15 or 30 years from now. We change and hopefully it is for the good.

What *career field* are you thinking about pursuing at this time?

What should be your major and what curriculum should you take? You can go back to Goal One and review Task Six and review what you wrote down with your academic advisor as your required courses and the electives you can take.

On the following pages, please list the courses you will be taking each year to meet your graduation target date. Monitor these courses so you do graduate on your target date and take the ones that can help you enter your chosen career field with a good job.

Taking The Right Courses to Graduate On Time and Land a Good Job

Date: Course Name	Freshman Year # of Hours	First Semester Final Grade
1. _____		
2. _____		
3. _____		
4. _____		
5. _____		
6. _____		
7. _____		
8. _____		

Date: Course Name	Freshman Year # of Hours	Second Semester Final Grade
1. _____		
2. _____		
3. _____		
4. _____		
5. _____		
6. _____		
7. _____		
8. _____		

Taking The Right Courses to Graduate On Time and Land a Good Job- Continued

Date: Course Name	Sophomore Year # of Hours	First Semester Final Grade
1.		
2.		
3.		
4.		
5.		
6.		
7.		
8.		

Date: Course Name	Sophomore Year # of Hours	Second Semester Final Grade
1.		
2.		
3.		
4.		
5.		
6		
7		
8.		

Taking The Right Courses to Graduate On Time and Land a Good Job-Continued

Date: Course Name	Junior Year # of Hours	First Semester Final Grade

1. _____

2. _____

3. _____

4. _____

5. _____

6. _____

7. _____

8. _____

Date: Course Name	Junior Year # of Hours	Second Semester Final Grade

1. _____

2. _____

3. _____

4. _____

5. _____

6 _____

7 _____

8. _____

Date: Course Name	Senior Year # of Hours	First Semester Final Grade
1.		
2.		
3.		
4.		
5.		
6.		
7.		
8.		

Date: Course Name	Senior Year # of Hours	Second Semester Final Grade
1.		
2.		
3.		
4.		
5.		
6		
7		
8.		

131

Taking The Right Courses to Graduate On Time and Land a Good Job-Continued

Date: Course Name	Fifth Year/Grad School # of Hours	First Semester Final Grade
1.		
2.		
3.		
4.		
5.		
6.		
7.		
8.		

Date: Course Name	Fifth Year/Grad School # of Hours	Second Semester Final Grade
1.		
2.		
3.		
4.		
5.		
6		
7		
8.		

Task Two
Know the Challenges Facing You after Graduation so You Can Use Your College Education to Prepare for Them

You will be facing many challenges when you graduate from college. These include:

- Becoming Financially Secure
- Job Security
- Retirement
- Working in a Diverse Work Environment
- Finding a Company that Cares for it's Employees
- Career Transitioning

Financial Security

✓ Many college graduates are starting their careers with major debt. Much of the research indicates ex-undergraduate and graduate students might be $15,000-$100,000 in debt. How do you pay off this college debt quickly?

✓ The fact that college graduates are taking longer to secure a job adds more financial stress to the individual as well as his/her family. How do college graduates find a secure job today that pays well?

Job Security

✓ Over 40 million people are changing jobs every year and work for six to 15 different companies. It used to be if your changed job every three years, you were considered a job hopper and no one wanted to hire you. A person changing jobs every three years is the norm today. How do you find a job and keep it for five years or longer?

✓ People are living longer so they will be retiring later in life. This means the older person will keep his/her job longer and compete with college graduates for jobs.

Retirement

✓ The United States of America is becoming trillions of dollars in debt because of war and natural disasters. Where will the money come from in the future to pay for unemployment, social security, Medicare, Medicaid and government pension funds if the US government doesn't fund these programs?

✓ People can't depend on company pension funds for their retirement anymore. Individuals must start saving in their early 20's and until they decide to retire. According to the Employee Benefit Research Institute in Washington D.C., 45% of workers today have less than $25,000 saved for retirement while 18% have $100,000 or more. Of the workers 55 and older, 29% have less than $25,000 put away while 36% have $100,000 or more in the bank.

Working in a Diverse Work Environment

- ✓ The work force is becoming more diversified. Workers young and old of different gender and race need to learn how to work together. The differences between one another need to be understood and an agreement should be reached that we all are here to help each other and the company to be successful. Does your company promote diversity?
- ✓ Women will be challenging men for the top jobs in America. Today only six women are CEOs of Fortune 500 companies. However, this will change. 56% of the college graduates today are women and more are going to graduate school. Many women want to have a career and children and they are finding ways to do both. High school girls are now winning more academic awards and filling more school leadership positions then men. How will competition be between the sexes in the future?

Finding a Company that Cares for it's Employees

- ✓ We are becoming the country of the rich and poor. Many CEOs make 300 to 500 times the normal worker. CEOs strive to keep shareholders happy. You should find a CEO that wants to keep all stakeholders happy.
- ✓ Identify the companies that are given the best company to work for awards.
- ✓ Review privately held companies and public held companies both small and large until you find a company with the right people values and philosophy

Career Transitioning You should always be asking yourself the following seven questions in every career position whether just starting out or have been there for awhile.

- ✓ Are the performance expectations of me by my boss realistic?
- ✓ Do I have the authority and resources to achieve my boss's performance expectations of me?
- ✓ Is my working relationship with my boss, peers and direct reports good?
- ✓ Am I stagnant in my position?
- ✓ Do people like me and view me as a team player?
- ✓ Am I viewed as someone who gets things done and carrying his/her share of the load?
- ✓ Is the communication between me and my boss, peers, and direct reports good

By learning to think and make good decisions in college, you will be able to plan better and manage these changes in the years ahead.

Task Three
Develop a Plan on What You are Going to Do During the College Years to Build a Resume that will Land You a Job

You need to develop a resume and marketing letters focused on your career and job target. See Appendix A (sample resumes) and Appendix B (sample letters). You can also go online to the websites listed below to receive help in writing your resume.

- Online Writing Lab (OWL) Purdue University
    owl.english.purdue.edu/owl
- The Damn Good Resume
    damngood.com
- The Resume Place
    resume-place.com
- Susan Ireland
    Susanireland.com

We also recommend that you go to your local college career center or library to receive help in writing a resume that focuses on your career field/position target. A resume reflects your experiences and what you have done in high school and college. Employers want to know if you can do the job and work well with others. You should plan each year on what you are going to accomplish in college to build a resume that will sell you.

Each year, ask yourself the following questions.
What organizations will I join on campus?
What leadership positions will I fill on campus and elsewhere?
What community activities will I participate in?
What internships will I obtain this summer or winter?
Which languages will I master in college?
Will I practice the language in a country where they speak it?
Will I get involved in local and national government in any way?
What grade point average will I obtain in my major and overall?
What academic honors do I want to obtain?
What other honors do I want to obtain that would make me look good?
Please read *Appendix A*. It discusses the types of resumes and has examples.

Task Four
Develop a Job Search Plan and Start to Implement It Your Freshman Year so You Obtain Interviews and a Good Job Offer at Graduation

Six Tips to Help College Students Conduct an Effective Job Search Campaign and Find Employment.

Tip One- You should work closely with the college or university where you are obtaining or will obtain your degree or degrees.

- Professors at universities and colleges should be able to put you in touch with alumni who majored in your subject and now work in key positions at particular companies, firms or organizations.
- Many community colleges, universities and liberal arts colleges are not only partnering with companies to get their students hired but are helping American companies be more competitive in the world. It is a win- win situation for everyone.
- The college career centers will be posting jobs on their college website and bringing employers to campus. The college should have a list of alumni who can help graduates get in their company or organization.

Tip Two-Develop and Execute the ABC Network Model

One of the best ways to learn about a job openings or to meet someone who can hire you is through personal contacts. The A-B-C Network Model in a networking process that has been used by thousands of our clients. You list five to 10 people you know really well and put them in your A group. The A group then introduces you to people they know who can help you and this is the B group.

The B group then introduces you to people they know which is called the C group. You can have over 100 people on your list before you know it. In the end, you want to put people on your network list that can hire you or get you an interview. In essence, you want to network your way to the hiring managers in companies and organizations.

Listed on the next page is a list of places where can start contacting people. Create your A-team first and then your *B- team* and your *C-team last.*

Personal Contacts and People Who Perform Services-Put Names in Computer

Fellow Class Mates
Business associates
Personal friends
Your Parents
Parents of Fellow Students
Relatives
Friends of the family
Parents of your friends
Neighbors
Church members
Club contacts
Professors/teachers
School administrators
Members of your fraternity or sorority
Alumni (both high school and
college)
Past or present employers
Professional associations
Search firms
Accountant
Banker
Barber/Hairstylist
Dentist/Physician
Clergyman
Financial counselor
Lawyer
Local merchants
Insurance agent
Optometrist
Private Equity Firms
Politicians
Stockbrokers
Chamber of Commerce
Service clubs
State employment agency

Can you think of other people to put on the list?

Group A

List the name, job title/company, telephone number and e-mail of each person in your <u>A</u> group.

Name	Job Title/Company	Phone #	E-Mail
1.			
2.			
3.			
4.			
5.			
6.			
7.			
8.			
9,			
10.			
11.			
12.			

Group B

List the name, job title /company, telephone number and e-mail of each person in your <u>B</u> group.

	Name	Job Title/Company	Phone #	E-Mail
1.				
2.				
3.				
4.				
5.				
6.				
7.				
8.				
9,				
10.				
11.				
12.				

Group C

List the name, job title/company, telephone number and e-mail of each person in your C group.

	Name	Job Title/Company	Phone #	E-Mail
1.				
2.				
3.				
4.				
5.				
6.				
7.				
8.				
9,				
10.				
11.				
12.				

Tip Three-_Organize Your Career Advancement College Networking Team_

You should create career advancement networking teams to help you find the first position and the ones down the road as well. Each team should have six to eight members and each person's role is to help members find job leads, obtain interviews and advance their career. The team should select a coordinator to keep the group active and together. This coordinating position would rotate among members each year. You can start out with a career advancement college major networking team first and then develop one in graduate school and another as part of a professional organization you join. You can communicate to one another on linkedin, by e-mail, skype or by a conference call. The key to success is good and continuous communication.

The _Career Advancement Networking Teams_ can be organized as follows:

> Team #1 – By major in sorority/fraternity or major in undergraduate school
> Team #2 – Graduate or professional school classmates
> Team #3 – Members of the same professional association or honorary society

Please record your Career Advancement College Networking team name and list of members below:

Career Advancement Networking Teams

Team #1 (Group name :_____)

	Names	Present Employer	Phone #	E-Mail
1)				
2)				
3)				
4)				
5)				
6)				
7)				
8)				

Team #2 (Group name :_____)

	Names	Present Employer	Phone #	E-Mail
1)				
2)				
3)				
4)				
5)				
6)				
7)				
8)				

Team #3 (Group name :_____)

	Names	Present Employer	Phone #	E-Mail
1)				
2)				
3)				
4)				
5)				
6)				
7)				
8)				

You should approach networking like farming crops. You gently plant the seed in face-to-face meetings. You continually contact individuals once a month or more often, keeping them up-to-date and collecting more information and ideas (watering and keeping weeds away). If you continue to give them some attention, your network list, leads and high stress interviews will grow. The more face -to-face meetings with people in your network in the beginning, the more individuals will work for you. However, it is becoming more difficult to meet with people because they are doing two jobs at work now days.

You can take advantage of your network by identifying companies where you might like to work and then asking people in your network if they know anyone at those companies. You can network yourself to the door of the hiring manager.

Tip Four- Identify and Contact People in Companies Who Can Hire You And Use the Controlled Blitz Approach

You should work with professionals at your local library to identify companies where you want to work and executives in those organizations who can hire you. Community and college libraries spend a lot of money today to build data bases to help individuals find companies and hiring executives. You should take advantage of this service. In addition, the library usually has excellent computers you can use to e-mail letters and resumes to the mangers who can hire you. Start making a list of the companies where you might like to work and the executives in the company that can hire you. You can use Reference USA, the Million Dollar Directory, Lexis Nexis Library Express.

	Company Name	**Hiring Executive**	**Phone Number**
1.			
2.			
3.			
4.			
5.			
6.			
7.			
8.			
9.			
10.			
11.			
12.			

Company Name	Hiring Executive	Phone Number
13.		
14.		
15.		
16.		
17.		
18.		
19.		
20.		
21.		
22.		
23.		
24.		
25.		
26.		
27.		
28.		
29.		
30.		
31.		
32.		
33.		
34.		
35.		
36.		
37.		
38.		
39.		
40.		

You can put this list together. You can learn from someone who works at the library on how to gather data from these data bases. Once the list of companies is compiled, ask your network to review the list and give you the names of people that they know who works in each company. The mind works like a computer. If you say who works at this company that you might know? People can be of more helpful as you can place a name with something.

Use the Control Blitz Approach on Your Own to Set Up Interviews
The following is a seven phase control blitz approach you can use to obtain interviews with hiring managers and executives.

Phase One- Identify the hiring executives or managers of the companies you would like to contact and obtain their phone numbers, addresses and e-mails.

Phase Two- Write a letter and address it to the appropriate person of your identified companies and mail it with a copy of your resume. You might want to call the company first to make sure the appropriate person is still in his/her position and the address is accurate.

Phase Three- You should be sure to put in the letter that you will be calling them in four or five days. You should emphasize that you can help the hiring executive or manager accomplish his or her business goals and tell them about your strengths. You should send out five to eight letters a day and follow up four days later with the phone call. If the person's assistance asks is he/she expecting your call, you can truthfully say yes because you wrote that you would call.

Phase Four- You shouldn't send out more than eight letters a day because you will not be able to follow up adequately. Just think after one month, you will have contacted 100 to 200 companies and hopefully you will have had at least 10 meetings with the appropriate hiring mangers.

Phase Five- The control blitz approach calls for control of your calendar so you know when and where and what time these meetings will take place.

Phase Six- You should use the needs assessment sales approach when you meet with the hiring executive. You should prepare a series of thought provoking questions for the hiring person. In the end, you want the hiring manger to realize that he/she needs you. Their question is can we afford you? Your question is can you afford to let me get away?

Phase Seven- You might start with smaller companies at first because they do more hiring at this time than the big companies. If you use a name of a person in your network to contact the hiring manager, you will have a better chance of being interviewed and hired.

Tip Five-*Use online Job Search Websites*

The following are online job search websites you can use to identify job opportunities.

- ✓ America's Job Exchange-(americasjobexchange.com)-the successor to America's job exchange
- ✓ After College-(aftercollege.com)- This is a service for college students and recent graduates who are looking for entry-level jobs, internships or other opportunities in the USA or Canada.
- ✓ Career Builder-(careerbuilder.com)-Career Builder has evolved into one of the larger and more dynamic sites for job and career information.
- ✓ Career Matrix-(careermatrix.com)-You can search for jobs by category, keyword and location.
- ✓ College Grad Job Hunter-(collegegrad.com)
- ✓ EmploymentGuide.com
- ✓ Future step from Korn/Ferry (futurestep.com)
- ✓ Hotjobs.yahoo.com
- ✓ Indeed (indeed.com)
- ✓ Job Bank USA (jobbankusa.com)
- ✓ Job-hunt.org
- ✓ Jobstar.org
- ✓ Manpower (www.manpower.com)
- ✓ Monster.com
- ✓ MonsterTrak.com
- ✓ NationJob.com
- ✓ Net-temps.com
- ✓ Recruitersonline.com
- ✓ Rileyguide.com
- ✓ Snagajob.com
- ✓ Topechelon.com
- ✓ Go to websites of companies for job postings
- ✓ Linkedin- recruiters look for people on this website
- ✓ Facebook

We would recommend you buy a book called *Internet Job Searching* by Margaret Riley Dikel and Francis E. Roehm. Check on Amazon.com. They have identified all the websites to help people in career planning and finding employment.

Tip Six-You should Obtain Help from Professional Organizations

One of the first things many individuals think about when starting a job search is "Where can I go for professional help?" With so many people competing in the job market, it is important to take advantage of all the professional resources you can identify. The following is a list of professional resources and my viewpoint on them.

College Career Counseling Center

This is a good place to stay in touch if you need help in deciding on a career goal. You can take tests and explore the results with a qualified counselor. If you are a student, there is usually no charge. If you are a member of the community, the charge, if any, is usually very minimal.

Community College Library

Librarians are trained professionals who can help you identify all sorts of resources. They help job hunters every day so they know what is useful. Their services are also provided at no extra charge. Many of the libraries have spent money to buy data bases and conduct job search seminars for individuals.

State and Federal Government Agencies

Check with the state employment office to learn of advertised positions and how they can help you. Since the government is one of the largest employers in the United States, you can apply for a position in the state government, federal government, or the military.

Private or Temporary Employment Agencies

An employment agency is an organization, or person, who solicits job listings directly from employers for the purpose of earning a referral commission. They normally work with positions under $60,000. Employers give them specific information on job openings, including the job description and income range. The employers in turn become obligated to pay the agency a commission if they hire someone based on the agency's referral.

Mulligan & Associates- A Career Management Consulting Firm

If you need career counseling and coaching, you can call Mulligan & Associates at 847 981-5725. Maybe we can help you. We do charge a small hourly fee. We don't want to take the place of your college career center but we have helped over 10,000 individuals with career planning and finding employment and have a solid network like your college.

Task Five
Identify the Work Factors that are Important to You
in the Position That You are Pursuing.

Review the 25 factors below in regard to what is important to you in your next position. Rank the following 25 factors 1 highest– 25 lowest so you know what to look for when taking your next job.

1. Authority: How much position power will the company give me to get the job done?

2. Compensation package: Salary, bonus, insurance, stock options, car, country club, etc.

3. Location: What is the commuting time? In what part of the country is the job located?

4. Independence: How much will I be supervised?

5. Team orientation: A team atmosphere in which people work closely together.

6. Type of industry: Is the company in a growth industry?

7. Professional growth: Does the company offer in-house training programs and compensate continuing education?

8. Travel: How much time will I be on the road?

9. Time: How much time will I spend on various work tasks?

10. Flexible work hours: How many hours per week will I work? Can I alter my work schedule to meet my family situation?

11. Supervisor: Can I learn from him/her? Can I work with and for this person?

12. Work environment/culture: Formal or more laid back? Progressive or conservative?

13. Personality chemistry: Does my personality fit in with most of the personalities of the people in the department/office/firm?

14. Physical labor vs. mental work: Will I be using my mind or doing things physically?

15. Opportunity for advancement: Does the company have a career development succession planning program?

16. A company with a mentoring program for top performers and high potentials

17. Accumulating wealth.

18. Becoming an expert leader in my field.

19. Receiving recognition for my work.

20. Having time for leisure.

21. Being able to work creatively.

22. Having daily contact with people.

23. Doing something socially significant.

24. Being in a fast-paced environment with other competitive people.

25. Knowing I can depend on some certainty in the job.

Task Six
Prepare for Interviews and How to Negotiate so You Obtain Job Offers.

You need to know how to interview and negotiate to obtain an offer. We will cover the following topics on interviewing.

✓ A Pre-Interview Checklist
✓ Researching the Company
✓ Checking Your Appearance
✓ Plan Your Arrival
✓ Points to Remember during the Interview
✓ Avoid these Knock Out Factors
✓ Typical Interviewing Questions
✓ Questions to Ask the Interviewer
✓ Three Factors to Focus on During the Interview
✓ Negotiating the Offer

A Pre-Interview Checklist

Have you:

- Confirmed the time, place, and date of the interview?
- Studied all relevant literature and articles about the employer and persons interviewing you?
- Prepared yourself to answer the commonly asked questions?
- Reviewed the specific questions you want to ask during the interview?
- Considered your specific salary requirements?
- Listed the information you want to obtain from the interview?
- Dressed appropriately for the interview?

Researching the Company

You will have more confidence if you know more about the company prior to your first interview. This information helps you ask pertinent questions and carry on a intelligent dialogue with the interviewer.
Go to the library and use the following resources.

- Reference USA
- Million Dollar Directory
- Lexis Nexis Library Express
- Plunkett Research
- Business Source Premier

Listed below are some areas of a company you should research. Your librarian can help you locate information on businesses.

- Publicly or privately owned. Product-or service-oriented.
- Sales volume for the past five years. Profitability.
- History of management--recent turnover. Recent cutbacks of staff.
- Major markets
- Credit rating?
- History of acquisition?
- Recent articles on the company
- List of Officers and their backgrounds

Checking Your Appearance

Always be aware of the image you are presenting. To improve your self-confidence, wear an outfit in which you feel comfortable. Purchase the best garments you can afford; they are an investment in your future.

It is always safest to dress conservatively for the first interview. If at this interview you observe that your mode of dress is highly inappropriate, you can modify it for the next interview. Both men and women should have a navy or gray suit, preferably all wool, but a wool-polyester blend is satisfactory. Shirts can be all cotton or a polyester-cotton blend, either white or light blue, with long sleeves. Shoes should be conservatively cut; either black or cordovan leather is appropriate.

Men: Ties should be solid-color, diagonal stripe, or small-figured, and preferably silk. Hair should be neat, clean, combed, and appropriately styled for business--no way-out hairdos. If you wear a beard or mustache, it should be neat, well-trimmed, and nothing too extreme (no goatees, handlebars, etc.).

Women: Maintain a conservative posture on your hair and nails. No bright nail colors, please! Wear a minimum amount of make-up, perfume, jewelry and perfume.

Plan Your Arrival

The following suggestions are intended to help you be more confident prior to the interview.

- Make sure you get enough sleep the night before.
- Allow enough time to get to your destination promptly. If you arrive 15 to 20 minutes early, you can take time to freshen up before your interview. You don't want to appear disheveled and out of breath when you walk in.
- If it appears that you are going to be late, call the interviewer and let him or her know.
- Leave the overcoat and boots in the outer office.
- While in the reception room, try to relax and be positive. Read the annual report.
- Put your resume in a place where it will not be crumpled or smudged.
- Be pleasant and courteous to the receptionist or secretary. You never know when the boss will ask this person for input.

Points to Remember During the Interview ©

1. Walk toward the person confidently, shake hands and sit where he/she wants you to be.
2. Don't begin the interview with a negative remark, such as "It is sure stuffy in here, or "This is certainly a difficult place to get to or some other personal observation which may put the interviewer on the defensive.
3. Show a smile; don't come in and look like you just lost your best friend or look too serious.
4. Don't take a lot of things (portfolio, papers, briefcase, etc.) with you to the interview; an extra resume is, however, permissible.
5. Never argue with the interviewer.
6. Don't bring up salary, benefits, etc. If asked what you were earning, use general terms. "I was earning in the mid-forties." Emphasize the importance of the job and not the money until you get the offer. Remember, companies do give signing bonuses and early performance reviews.
7. Try to fix the interviewer's name in your mind, and use it occasionally during the conversation. Everybody likes to hear the sound of his or her name.
8. Don't chew gum or smoke during the interview.
9. Make it a point to look at the interviewer as you speak or listen. Meet him eye to eye.
10. Speak distinctly. Don't mumble or go into a detailed account of gripes and grievances.
11. Don't give excuses for past failures. Answer all questions honestly and show how you have actually benefited by some of your previous mistakes.
12. .After the interview, be sure to thank the interviewer sincerely for his or her time. Follow up with a written thank-you and e-mail.

Avoid These "Knock-Out Factors"

Every interviewer has a personal "list" of taboos that will disqualify a job applicant. The following list of taboos, or "knock-out factors," was submitted by human resource executives from over 150 large corporations:

- ✓ Poor personal appearance
- ✓ Overbearing, conceited, superiority complex; a "know-it-all" attitude
- ✓ Inability to express oneself clearly; poor voice, diction, or grammar
- ✓ Lack of planning for a career; no purpose or goal
- ✓ Lack of confidence and poise; nervousness
- ✓ Overemphasis on money
- ✓ Poor educational record
- ✓ Lack of courtesy; ill-mannered
- ✓ Failure to look interviewer in the eye
- ✓ No sending e-mails doing interview
- ✓ Limp handshake
- ✓ Sloppy application form
- ✓ Cynical outlook
- ✓ Inability to take criticism
- ✓ Tardiness
- ✓ Failure to express appreciation for the interviewer's time
- ✓ Smell of smoke on you-Smoking too much

Preparing to Sell Yourself

You need to sharpen your interviewing skills so you feel comfortable in selling yourself. Perhaps the biggest obstacle to interviewing effectively is the inability to talk about oneself. This inability is a conditioned process and is regarded as the major reason people undersell or don't sell themselves.

Many employers say students have two glaring weaknesses.
- **Students do not have a clear picture of their career path.**

An example of what you can say.

Interviewer: "What are you looking for in a position?"

You- "I am seeking a position where I can grow personally, professionally and help the company meet it's business objectives. The position you outlined appears to present that opportunity."

Interviewer: "Where do you want to be in five years?"

You- "A move up the career ladder or more responsibilities in my present position. I do have a career management model that I execute. It calls for me setting a yearly and five year career position target. However, there are a couple of key factors to whether or not I can advance and those factors are my boss and the company. Right now I would like to start in the position you have available and work with my boss to identify my next position".

- **Students do not interview well. They are usually not prepared to answer the questions.**

We have found that the biggest weakness of people who interview for jobs is that their answers are usually too long. They don't practice their answers to questions ahead of time and they are not precise when giving an answer.

To assist you in this process, it is recommended that you use an audio tape. Sit down with a tape recorder, ask yourself questions and answer them like you would do during an interview. Keep refining your remarks on the tape until you are comfortable with your answers and expression. This audio preparation is an ideal tool for responding to open-ended or "sell" questions, such as "Tell me a little about yourself." What are your strengths and weaknesses? Why should we hire you? Give me an example of how you solved a problem. What were your results?

Another way to prepare yourself is to have someone interview you using audio video equipment. We would not send one of our clients to an interview without going through a filming session. You can see yourself struggling to find the right answer to a question and view your body language as well. You can ask someone from your college career center to film you and review your performance with you.

Typical Interview Questions Directed at College Graduates

- Describe your education for me.
- What is your major and why did you select it?
- What was your class standing?
- What campus activities did you participate in?
- What honors did you earn?
- What was your grade point average in your major and overall?
- Did your grades adequately reflect your full capability? Why not?
- What courses did you like best/least and why?
- Have you had any special training for this job I am discussing with you?
- Why are you interested in joining our company?
- What do you think you can do for us?
- Why did you select your college or university?
- How would you describe yourself?
- What are your long-range and short-range goals and objectives, when and why did you establish these goals, and how are you preparing to achieve them?
- What specific goals, other then those related to your occupation, have you established for yourself for the next five years?
- What do you really want to do in life?
- What are the most important rewards you expect in your career?
- Which is more important to you, the money or the type of job?
- What do you consider your greatest strengths and weaknesses?
- How do you think a friend or a professor who knows you well would describe you?
- What motivates you to put forth your greatest effort?
- How has your education prepared you for a career?
- Why should we hire you?
- What qualifications do you have that make you think that you'll be successful?
- How do you determine or evaluate success?
- What do you think it takes to be successful in a company like ours?
- What qualities should a successful manager possess?
- Describe your most rewarding college experience.
- If you were hiring a graduate for this position, what qualities would you look for?
- Describe the relationship that should exist between a supervisor and subordinates.
- Do you have plans for continued study? (Graduate students may be asked: Why did you decide to pursue an advanced degree?)
- How do you work under pressure?
- In what part-time or summer jobs have you been most interested? Why?
- What do you know about our company?
- Are you seeking employment in a company of a certain size? Why?
- What criteria are you using to evaluate the company for which you hope to work?
- Do you have geographical preferences? Why?
- Will you relocate?
- Are you willing to travel?
- What two or three things are most important to you in your job?
- What major challenge have you encountered and how did you deal with it?
- What have you learned from your mistakes?

Questions to Ask the Interviewer

- How do you or the organization work with new employees to help them get a good start?
- What is the CEO's vision for this company or organization?
- What is your vision for the department?
- What is your definition of leadership and how do you expect your people to lead?
- What are the major concerns that keep you up at night?
- On a scale of 1 to 10 (1 - lowest, 10 - highest), how do you rate the cohesiveness of the department and the company at this time?
- What are the three primary objectives of your department?
- How do you describe the culture of your department? the company?
- What significant changes to you foresee in the near future?
- What would be your expectation of me the first year? second year? third year?
- Do you like to write Performance Expectation PACs with your people so both of you know what you can expect from each other?
- What is your management philosophy in regard to balancing work, family and one's personal life?
- What would be my biggest challenges the first year on the job?
- How does the company like to reward high performing employees?
- How does the company select high potential employees?
- What do you do to help your direct reports grow?

Three Key Factors to Focus on During the Interview ©
There are three key factors to focus on in every interview: 1) establishing rapport with the interviewer -likeability 2) identify the challenge that faces the company and the person in that position-knowledge of industry and job 3) selling yourself based on what the employer wants and needs-In other words, you can perform the job. The "consulting" or "needs assessment" sales approach is the recommended procedure for an interview. The process focuses on establishing rapport, exploring and understanding the needs of the client or boss, and presenting you as someone who is the answer to solving problems and helping the boss & company be successful.

Establish Rapport
After years of research, social scientists have concluded that good interpersonal relationships require warmth, empathy, and respect. Show interest in the person and job..
Identify the Challenge
All good interpersonal relationships feature an exchange of information, whereby two people equally share the talking and listening. Try to establish a natural exchange of conversation.

Close the Deal-Negotiating Your Package
At the end of the conversation, rephrase what you heard the interviewer say the company needs from a person in the position you are applying, and tell him/her once more how you fit the specs and how you can help them. If you are not comfortable with the package they offer you and you want the job, ask if your package can be renegotiated after you have proven your worth.

154

Task Seven
Review What the Professionals Say are the
Key Factors to Career Advancement

We surveyed 10 professionals that we have been associated with for many years and asked them their opinions on what they think are the key factors in advancing one's career in today's work environment. Three served as a CEO/President, four worked as human resource officers and three were retained executive recruiters who recruit senior executives.

The CEOs and Presidents

Fred Florjancic, *Former CEO and President of Safety Kleen in Dallas, TX,* said:

The most significant factors in helping me advance in my career were:
1) Obtaining as much formal education as possible (I have a B.S. and MBA from Indiana University and an Advanced Management Degree from Harvard University).
2) Ambition, hard work, passion, knowing my strengths and weaknesses, and being adventuresome.
3) Being lucky – the right place at the right time.
4) Being blessed with a few key mentors along the way.

Dr. William Muse, *former President of Auburn University, University of Akron and East Carolina University, and Business Dean at Appalachian State University, Texas A&M and University of Nebraska at Omaha,* said:

The foundation of performance and advancement are:
1) Excellent communication skills – the ability to communicate orally and in writing.
2) Having effective interpersonal skills – the ability to get along with others.
3) Excellent decision making (analytical skills) - the ability to make good choices and decisions.
4) Drive, energy and motivation – the ability to get the job done.

Kathy Nauer, *President and Co-owner of Financial One, Inc., a privately held accounting firm servicing non-profit organizations,* said:

1) You can start out with another company, learn the business and then start your own company in the same industry. You can start a similar business if you don't have a non-compete clause in your contract.
2) A good business plan needs to be developed which includes your budget, **objectives** and a list of potential customers.
3) It helps to have a spouse making a good living so you can take a risk.
4) You have to be willing to work long hours to meet your customer needs and deadlines.
5) You have to keep your cash flow strong so you can sleep at night.

The Human Resource Officers

John Estrada, Former *Vice President of Human Resources of Motorola*, said people who want to advance must:

1) Know their skill sets and be able to communicate them to others.
2) Learn how to source out information and know their way around the company.
2) Build a network of supporters within the company.
3) Do what they can to attend workshops and classes to keep growing.

Bob Kasenter, *former Chief Human Resource Officer for Montgomery Ward and now Chief Human Resource Officer for EZ Corp*, said:

1) Education gets you in the door, but outstanding performance helps you keep your job.
2) A strong work ethic is extremely important. One should do every assigned task, no matter how big or small the best you can. No one should think an assignment by their boss is beneath them.
3) One needs intelligence to figure out what should be done next.
4) A person needs to be a good communicator in expressing himself. More people are promoted or fired based on how they communicate.

Bob Keith, *Senior Vice-President of Employee Relations at CNA Insurance*, said, employees should:

1) Be concentrating more on advancing the business than advancing themselves. This attitude will come through to others and career advancement will come in time.
2) Be passionate about the business and understand the business thoroughly.
3) Be independent thinkers and able to articulate their thoughts in a clear and concise manner.
4) Carefully understand the facts and think in the alternative – being able to recommend a number of solutions rather than just one.
5) Not spend time with a new boss defending the old way of doing things. One should be open to the new ways and methods of your boss.
6) Not forget that the important people in the equation are the customers and shareholders.

Andrea Skobel, Former *Chief Human Resource Executive John Crane, a manufacturing company*, said a person who wants to advance should:

1) Be able to see the big picture of what the company is trying to accomplish and how their job or role fits in.
2) Know how their department does what it does and ask how they can do it better.
3) Anticipate the needs of the customer today and tomorrow.
4) Drive for continuous improvement.

The Retained Executive Recruiters

Jim Drury, *Chairman and Chief Executive Officer of James Drury Partners,* said there are five factors essential to achieving maximum career success. These factors are:

Risk Taking - Trial and error is critically important to finding out what one is truly good at, and not good at. People aspiring to great success must have the risk profile to try new and different things to find career truth. Trial and error is the central part of the equation. People who are risk averse seldom achieve their maximum career potential.

Passion – The most successful people have an innate passion and desire to be so in their chosen field. Their excitement about the possibilities for the future is tangible. People can feel their passion, and it can inspire others. They are always moving with a sense of purpose in the direction of what they visualize career success to be. They are focused, and not easily diverted to other preoccupations that can distract them and waste their time. Time is of real value to them.

Resilience – The most successful people are able to rebound from adversity, rather than to become overwhelmed by it. They are able to overcome disappointment and failure. They learn from it, put it behind them, and move on with a renewed sense of energy and opportunity. While being practical, they nevertheless have an enthusiastic sense of optimism and expectation that propels them forward.

Right Place/Right Time – Many people think success is often a matter of being in the right place at the right time, and if they don't achieve success, it's easy to blame it on that factor. I would rephrase it to say it's being at "a right place at a right time," and there are many potential right places and right times in one's career, if one is proactively looking for them. Again, that means being open to change and willing to move in new directions and attempt new things in order to find career truth. I've often said that "finding one's destiny is a matter of progressively moving toward the light, and away from the dark." In other words, moving in the direction of spending more of your time doing those professional things that come naturally and that are done extraordinarily well, and away from those things that can be done, but with difficulty – and can only be done satisfactorily, at best. For example, that might mean that an engineer or scientist trained to think analytically ultimately becomes one of the world's best business strategists. Or it might mean that an artist who is very good, but not great, ultimately becomes one of the great art dealers or agents. It could mean that an accountant who likes people and ideas, but tires of just crunching numbers, becomes a great venture capitalist.

Superb Execution – Successful careers are about getting the job done. Many people never deliver on their commitments. They make promises that are never kept. Trust is based on fulfilling one's promises. It's very simple, but one ultimately achieves great success by achieving successes at many steps along the way. The best leaders typically emerge because they can be relied upon to come through with the good.

Mick Donahue, *President of Donahue Patterson*, said a recruiter looks for people that:

1) Have a successful track record – you have to prove that you can do the job that they are seeking.
2) Have the ability to sell yourself to ypur boss colleagues, direct reports, and customers.
3) Have intellect and the ability to solve problems.
4) Have the right education, training and credentials for the job. It is the tie breaker between two people.

Andrew Nugent, *Former President of Lake Forest Executive Search*, said the keys to career advancement are:

1) Think like you are self-employed. It doesn't matter if you're running UBS or McKinsey, you're in charge of running your career. Start acting like it.
2) Learn how to play well with others. No one likes an arrogant person– even top performers start to wear thin.
3) Shut up. Men average 2,000 words per day; women average 7,000. Both those numbers could be halved. The more you talk, the less an impact you're making.
4) Move before it's time (Jack Welch). Moral hazard argument – good people leave. Top performers don't stay in one place for fifteen years.
5) Get outside your comfort zone – it will make you more interesting.

Dr. Mulligan reiterates the six career factors that he thinks are key to career advancement and they are:

1) Who you know – the people in your circle of life.
2) What you know – education, experience, job and industry knowledge, skills and how to work with and through people to establish objectives and achieve them.
3) How you are perceived as a leader, follower, performer and as being someone your boss, peers and direct reports can trust and count on.
4) How you do – your past performance and reputation for helping the company save, obtain and make money so all stakeholders win.
5) Obtaining job titles in companies so you can move forward in your career. For example, it is difficult to be recruited as a CFO if you have never held the title of CFO. It is important to pick up a title which moves you up the career ladder.
6) Staying in touch with executive recruiters and developing and communicating with a career advancement college networking team is extremely important.

In summary, the 10 professionals and Dr. Mulligan all mentioned important factors that have to do with career advancement. It is recommended that you review what these individuals had to say with your career counselor at college and your mom and dad and discuss them.

APPENDIX A
RESUMES

In Appendix A, we will define resume, discuss what a resume should do, identify three types of resumes and provide you with examples in each category.

What is a resume?
A resume is a concise personalized statement of your qualifications, job titles, responsibilities, accomplishments, education and special skills and honors which describes you and sells you in the job market and to your network.

What should a resume do?
A resume must catch the attention of potential employers and create a favorable first impression. It should allow employers to view you as a potential employee, thereby asking you in for an interview. When you develop a resume, it helps you understand your work history, accomplishments, and the special skills that you have developed over time. This acquired knowledge of yourself helps build your confidence so you don't "undersell" yourself to your network or in an interview.

What Are the Types of Resume Formats?
There are as many different types of resumes as there are experts. However, for simplicity sake, we suggest you use one of the following:
1)   The chronological resume
2)   The functional resume
3)   The functional/chronological resume
Examples of each type of resume are given in this Appendix

The **Chronological Resume.** The chronological resume focuses heavily on employment history, job responsibilities, accomplishments, and related experiences that support your career path. This format lists all of your occupations and employers, beginning with your most recent job. Do not list beginning jobs which were insignificant. How far back you go depends on what the first job adds to the resume. The chronological resume is the most common and easiest to read, and the type most preferred by executive search firms and employers.

Advantages. If you have a progressive employment history without any questionable employment gaps or short-term jobs, this format will present you as a person with an upward career path. The chronological resume also is an excellent format if you are seeking a similar position in the same industry because it shows you have worked in the industry and tells what you have accomplished in the positions you have held.

Disadvantages. This type of resume can stereotype you, especially if you have had the same job title over the years. People might see you as filling only one to three positions and working in the same industry your total career. Because of the résumé's focus on employment history and job title, your skills and talents might not appear as strong and diversified as you would like. In addition, if you are just starting your career and haven't held many jobs, it is difficult to sell yourself using this format. It will also show your age more quickly than other resume formats, which can be a plus or minus depending on your present age. Individuals have a more difficult time switching career fields using the chronological resume.

The Functional Resume. The functional resume emphasizes your qualification summary, and then list three or four main areas/functions of your job description with your accomplishments and skills listed under area/function.. In the qualifications summary, you describe yourself as a Strategic Human Resource Executive with demonstrated accomplishments in compensation and benefits, employees relations, talent and leadership development and recruiting. You would list your accomplishments under the four functional areas that I just mentioned. You will not list your employment history on this resume.

Advantages. The functional resume hides a void in one's previous employment, emphasizing instead your accomplishment skills, potential, and other positives as it relates to the different areas of the job. You want to take the employer away from industry experience and have him/her focus on the fact you have great accomplishments and skills in the areas of the job you are seeking.. It also aids the jobseeker with little employment experience showing off certain strengths.

Disadvantages. Since the reader doesn't see anything about your chronological work experience, it could signal a "red flag." (Naturally, this disadvantage depends largely on the age and work experience of the individual.) Also, the reader is given little or no information about your accomplishments in the jobs and industries in which you worked.

The **Functional/Chronological Resume.** This resume is a mixture of both the functional and chronological formats. It lists functions and accomplishments first and reveals the employment history last.

Advantages. The combination/creative is the most complete resume. The reader receives a positive picture of your strengths in different work areas and then can review your employment history. This resume also presents you as a versatile individual, able to fill a variety of positions. In essence, you can arrange the content in a format that best sells you.

Disadvantages. Some employers might wish to read about what you did in each job, believing it provides them with a better picture of the scope of your responsibilities and achievements.

160

How Is a Resume Read?

A person who receives dozens--maybe hundreds--of resumes in response to a specific position reviews each resume in about 20 seconds. This first scan quickly identifies the "best" resumes and forms a smaller "potential candidate" pile, using some sort of personal checklist of "knock-out" factors. These resumes are then reviewed in greater depth. The screener, at this point, is usually looking for reasons not to include a resume in the final list of candidates. Resumes that provide such a reason are set aside and receive no further consideration.

If your resume makes it to the third stage, you will probably be contacted for an interview. The screener will begin to prepare specific questions for the interview process.

All interviewers tend to work from the resume during certain stages of the interview. The most effective resumes provide important and positive information for discussion and expansion.

How Is a Resume Evaluated?

The resume is usually evaluated according to three major criteria:

1) **Experience and Qualifications.** These include full-time and part-time work experience; related experience, acquired skills, personal skills and abilities, community work and educational background;
2) **Proven Track Record.** The best predictor of future performance is past performance. That is why you must portray your past performance effectively in your resume. Employers are also looking for certain skills and accomplishments so you want to put words in the resume that match the qualifications employers listed in their ads.
3) **Potential.** A person who reads your resume projects strengths about you and begins to form a general impression of you. Therefore, your resume must create a picture that matches your personality, attributes, appearance, and abilities. It must also describe what you did in your various jobs, not what a person in those jobs was responsible for doing.

How Is a Resume Developed?

One of the greatest challenges facing you as you write your resume is selecting the appropriate content (and knowing how to format it). Generally, you need two major areas of knowledge in order to develop the most appropriate resume- **self-knowledge** and **knowledge of position description**. .

Self-knowledge involves developing a list of all your past responsibilities, positions, accomplishments, education and honors won.

Knowledge of position description includes knowing exactly what past experience, accomplishments, skills, experience and personal characteristics they want in a person who is going to be in this job.

Listed below are a number of content areas that are included in a resume. Not all items are included in every resume, nor are they all included at the same time. Each will be discussed to help you decide what to include and what to omit. You may find that you should write two or even three resumes based on the job and industry target.

What to include in a resume:
- ❖ Personal Information
- ❖ Qualification Summary
- ❖ Education Credentials-Up Front if Recent
- ❖ Employment History- Titles and Dates
- ❖ Reported to and Responsibilities and Accomplishments
- ❖ Professional Activities
- ❖ Community Activities
- ❖ Honors/Extracurricular Activities
- ❖ Military service
- ❖ References

Personal Information. An employer might scan 400 to 1200 resumes for a single position. It is important, therefore, not to include any personal information that might prejudice the screener. Include only your name, address, telephone number(s) and e-mail. If you are attending college away from home, you may list both your home and school addresses and phone numbers and e-mail.

Don't include:
- ❖ References to height, weight, race, religious affiliation, health, or names and ages of children
- ❖ Salary desired or salary history (save this information until you talk to the employer)
- ❖ Leisure time activities (tennis, golf, etc.)
- ❖ The reason for changing jobs
- ❖ Marital status

Career Objective. Many people include their career objective in their resume. This is fine if you have narrowed your choice to a specific job or industry and feel certain of your decision. State clearly and concisely the entry level, the functional areas or department (accounting, personnel, sales, etc.), and the type of company and industry you are seeking. If you know, indicate your short-and long-range career goals. However, be aware that by being so specific you may also limit your job options and force yourself to keep several types of resumes on hand to send as the occasion demands. In the majority of cases, it is better to state your objective in the cover letter and develop a strong qualification summary positioning yourself in the market place with employers.

Qualification Summary. A qualification summary states precisely who you are and pinpoints the major skill areas in which you have the most accomplishments. This is your opportunity to describe your strengths in the beginning of the resume, with the remaining parts of the resume to support the statement. The qualification summary should be no more than three to six lines long and appear as the first topic after your name, address, phone number and e-mail. Some examples follow.

> An achievement-oriented liberal arts major who has demonstrated the ability to manage and lead others, to learn quickly, to work efficiently, and to plan and implement programs effectively.

> A competitive marketing major who has demonstrated accomplishments in strategy and organization, research, advertising, and sales promotion.

> Fifteen years of management experience utilizing my skills in planning, organization, communication, and managing others. (homemaker)

When writing a functional/chronological resume, the major functional areas should be listed in your qualification summary and then fully developed in the body of the resume in that order. The following example shows functional areas underlined to illustrate this point:

> Senior executive with demonstrated ability to accomplish profit turnarounds under a variety of industrial and organizational constraints. Major achievements in **retail operations, distribution, processing**, and **manufacturing**.

Education Credentials. Where you place your degrees and training on the resume depends largely on their importance and relevance to the position you are seeking and the strength of your credentials. It also depends on when you graduated. If you graduated within the last three or four years, put it up front. If you graduated 15 years ago, your experience and job titles win out.

Place your education credentials immediately following the qualification summary if:
- ❖ You are graduating from college or completing a training program, and your education or training relates directly to the jobs you are seeking
- ❖ You have a master's degree in management or an M.B.A. and you are applying for a management position
- ❖ You are a C.P.A. seeking a top financial position
- ❖ You have a Ph.D. and seek a position requiring that degree

Place your education credentials after your work experience if:
- ❖ Your degree and undergraduate work do not relate to your career goal.
- ❖ Your highest degree is a bachelor's and your work experience and work-related accomplishments will sell you better to prospective employers
- ❖ You have an M.A. or higher, but the position you seek isn't related to your credentials
- ❖ Your degrees are not recent. You graduated seven years ago or later.

This section should also include any and all relevant courses and training programs, including workshops, seminars, etc.

Employment History. This represents the most important part of the resume. Starting with your most recent job and moving back towards your first job, outline on a sheet of paper the name of each employer, the number of months or years spent in each position, your specific responsibilities, and what you accomplished in each job. If your employment history is progressive and shows depth, it should appear right after the qualification summary or early in the resume. If your work experience is limited, you might want to write a functional chronological resume.

Many people have difficulty writing their accomplishments, and this is due in part to natural modesty. The next step in this section will discuss accomplishments in detail and help you learn how to describe yours in a resume.

Professional Activities. These include research papers, presentations, organizations (as member, officer, etc.), publications, committees, conferences, or seminars (as attendee or worker).

Community Activities. If the activity is related or appropriate to your career objective, include it. For example, if you seek a job in the field of gerontology and you have developed and implemented a program in your community nursing home, this activity would appropriately fit into your resume.

Honors, Awards, and Extracurricular Activities. If you are a recent college graduate, most of your accomplishments will probably be listed in this section. Include them if they are recent and/or appropriate. If, however, you have been out of college for 20 years, in most instances your college awards would be too old to mention. However, if the award is related specifically to your field of interest or your career objective, it should be included.

Military Experience. If you are currently serving in the military or have served in the military, list your training and experience in such a way that it relates to the position you are seeking.

References. Your resume should simply state "Available upon request." Give the interviewer a copy of your references if requested during the interview.
about yourself:

When I attended a Midwest Association College and Employer meeting this Fall, Employers said they gave an A on most college graduate resumes. This means you do have to work on your resume and make it sure it sells you. You also need to know what is in your resume and be able to communicate it on the phone and in person. Therefore, don't let some fancy resume writer put a lot of flowery statements in your resume that you don't know anything about doing.

As previously mentioned , there are three types of resumes: **chronological, functional,** and **functional/chronological**. Each has its own advantage. Examples of each type are presented here with some biographical information on the fictitious resume subjects to explain his or her resume choice.

The **Chronological Resume**-As its name suggests, the chronological resume presents work experience in chronological order, from most recent to your first job.

MIKE SMITH- Mike's work experience included working in jobs that paid his way through college. He played up his accomplishments in sports and his competitive nature since he wanted to go into sales.

BRAD ZIMMERMAN:-Brad's resume was created to help him obtain an internship.

LINDA K. FANNELLI:-Linda had exceptional accomplishments but few activities when she worked as a computer aide and manager of operations, so a chronological resume was in order.

ANNE E. VALENTINE:-Anne wanted to work in public relations with a theatre or in a company in a large city. She wrote a chronological resume without a qualification summary. She decided to put her career objective in the letters she sent with her resume.

WILLIAM LOCKPORT is just graduating from college and wants to get a job with a private equity firm. He has tried to work in internships that would help him obtain a job in that industry.

DAVID JONES graduated from a weekend executive MBA program and has 12 years of work experience in the leisure industry. He prepared a chronological resume but he is having difficulty in changing industries.

DONALD GILCHRIST wants to go in the transportation industry after graduation and has done a nice job of obtaining internships along the way. The chronological resume is the right one for him.

AMY L. SMITH:- is expecting her second child and decided to take a year off from teaching. She developed this resume to obtain tutoring assignments. She plans to return to teaching in two years

M. MARGARET O'CONNOR: Margaret felt comfortable in stating a career objective. It was backed by a progressive employment history with fair accomplishments. The results of her achievements could have been quantified more, but she didn't keep records.

Michael V. Smith

Xxx Smith St., Mt. Prospect, IL 60006 Cell: (888)999-5555 E-mail: mv123@gmail.com

Profile	Results oriented Liberal Arts student (major "History", minor "Science") who wants to work in sales and marketing and help his company be number one in the marketplace. **Major Strengths:** • Competitive • Determined • Self Directed • Wants to play for a manager who can build a champion team • Excellent communicating skills • A strategist • A problem solver • Strong math skills • Can lead and follow • Strong work ethic
Objective:	**Target Position:** • A sales position **Industry:** • Pharmaceutical • Sports/Entertainment • Finance/Banking **Company:** • Size – no choice at this time • Culture – believe happy employees generate more customers and better service • Geography – Midwest
ALMA College achievements 2011-2015	• Played on ALMA'S 2014 MIAA Baseball Championship Team. • All MIAA Baseball in 20013 and 2014. 2014 MIAA Batting Champion at .408 and 3rd in country for home runs in Division three – Captain of baseball team. • Played defensive half back 2009. Intercepted six passes – voted 2nd team all MIAA. • Served as Resident Advisor in Resident Hall 20013-14 • Served as Chaplain and Scholarship chairman of TKE fraternity in 2013. • Voted Athlete of the Year in 2013-14.
Algonac High Achievements 2006-2011	• 2006-2010 played on five championship teams – three in baseball, one in football and one in basketball. • All conference in football, basketball and baseball and captain of all three teams senior year. • Co-President of Student Council senior year. • St. Clair County Sportsmanship Award in football.
Work History Summer 2014 Senior Year 20013-14 Summer 2013 Junior Year Summer 2012 Summer 2011 Pre - Freshman	• Athletic Director at Camp Waldron, Laconia, New Hampshire • Resident Advisor • Janitor in Old Main Building – 2 hours a day after football and baseball practice • Worked for Chris Craft Corporation in Fiber Glass Department • Study Hall Proctor at local High School, Assistant Physical Education teacher 3 hours a day at local Jr. High School • Construction worker • Houseman at Resort on Harsens Island, Michigan • Worked as Bus Boy on weekend and umpired little league games during week

166

Brad Zimmerman
Xxx South Ridge Ave.
Arlington Heights, Ill. 60005
888-999-5642
bradley.zimmerman@gmail.com

Internship Objective

Seeking an internship in the advertising and marketing field which will prepare me for employment after graduation. Strong work ethic with a desire to learn, grow and help others and the company be successful.

Education

Marquette University Milwaukee, WI   (Target Graduation May 2012)
- Currently enrolled in the College of Business Administration - Junior
- Double Major: Marketing - made Dean's List freshman year

St. Viator High School, Arlington Heights, IL   Graduation: May 2006
- Special Olympics, four year starter in basketball and captain of the team

Skills

Microsoft Professional XP, Power Point, Excel, Word, communication skills, leader, team player, and excellent customer service.

Employment History

IGL Real Estate   Wildwood, IL   Summer 2009 and 2010
Desk Secretary/Cleaning Assistant
Answered phone calls on a daily basis helping customers with problems and concerns. Also focused on maintaining a clean environment to make a positive impression on customers.

Peters Decorating, Inc.   Arlington Heights, IL   Summer 2008 and 2009
Assistant
Helped this organization make profit by doing a good job of cleaning walls, painting and being polite to customers. Work was completed in hospitals, office buildings and homes.

Car Detailing   Arlington Heights, IL   Summer 2008-
Entrepreneur – started a cleaning business
A friend and I purchased our own cleaning supplies and detailed cars for friends, neighbors, or anyone interested. We designed flyers and provided good customer service.

Northwest Metal Craft   Arlington Heights, IL   Summer 2007
Marketing Assistant
 Assisted in the creation and distribution of flyers that promoted the store's products and services Increased business by 20%

LINDA K. FANNELLI
Xxx S. Hamilton
Melrose Park, Illinois 60473
(999) 555-1234
ekfannelli@gmail.com

QUALIFICATIONS

A computer programmer who has demonstrated the ability to listen and understand individual problems, code specific programs, and consult and manage people.

EDUCATION

A.A.S. Triton College, Melrose Park, Illinois (Graduated June 2014)

PROGRAMMING SKILLS

- BASIC Language
- RPG Language

- COBOL Language
- BASIC Assembler Language

EMPLOYMENT HISTORY

February 2013-   TRITON COLLEGE - MELROSE PARK, ILLINOIS
   Present   Computer Lab Aide

- Coordinated the coding and debugging of programs. Directly responsible for over 175 programs being completed.
- Taught the operational procedures of the IBM system to 300 people.
- Maintained a filing system for all programs. Reduced theft of programs by 50 percent.
- Mounted and dismounted tape drives. Enabled individuals to run their own programs.
- Served as a consultant to all people who needed assistance.
- Operated card readers and keypunch machines.

March 2011   CORRIGAN ELECTRICAL SUPPLY COMPANY - PALOS HILLS, ILLINOIS
   to present   Manager of Operations

- Recruited, trained, and scheduled the work of the staff. Reduced turnover by 30 percent.
- Developed a system to maintain needed inventory supplies. Saved time and reduced costs by five percent.

RERERENCES

Available upon request

Anne Elizabeth Valentine
Xxx East Mayfair   (888) 999--6666Cell
Arlington Heights, Illinois 60005 aevalentine@hotmail.com

EDUCATION
Denison University, Granville, OH
Majors: English and Dance
- Tamalpa Institute Dancers Workshop; San Francisco, CA
- Gus Giordano Studios; Evanston, IL
- Lou Conte Studios; Chicago, IL

WORK EXPERIENCE includes internships in Communication, Advertising, and Event Planning
Student Coordinator (September 2014-Present)
Denison University Dance Department, Granville, OH
Assisted dance department head in coordinating and organizing the American College Dance Festival Association (Northeast region) conference for 300 professionals from 24 colleges and universities. Scheduled master classes, adjudications and scholarship auditions for dance department, as well as choreographing and performing own work.

Communications Coordinator (May 2013 – June 2014)
Mulligan & Associates, Inc., Chicago, IL
Edited/proofread resumes and marketing letters for outplacement firm. Typing/filing/reception.

Internship (May 2014)
Waste Management, Oak Brook, IL
Wrote publicity material. Assisted in opening of the plastic recycling alliance.

Photographic Assistance (Summer 2013)
Heidrich & Blessing, Chicago, IL
Assisted photographers by making slides of their work, refining the final product.

Outdoor Tripper (Summer 2012)
Camp Lake Hubert, MN
Directed canoeing/hiking trips for girls ages 9-17 in the boundary waters of Minnesota and Canada.

Internship (May 2012
Carson Pirie Scott, Chicago, IL
Wrote articles for internal newsletter.

Teacher (Summer 2011
Kindercare, Buffalo Grove, IL
Worked with infant through preschool children in day care chain. Taught various activities.

Internship (January 2011)
Foote Cone & Belding Advertising Agency, Chicago, IL
Worked in creative department developing ideas for Kraft Bull's Eye Barbecue Sauce.

HONORS, ACHIEVEMENTS AND ACTIVITIES
Denison University
- Fellow, Dance Department – Taught community and college level classes
- Advocate counselor for rape/sexual assault services
- Co-Director of Denison University Recycling Projects
- Volunteer for New Beginnings (battered women shelter), Granville, OH

WILLIAM P. LOCKPORT
Xxx FOREST LANE Park Ridge, IL 60093
(847) 999-1428   wlockport@gmail.com

EDUCATION

SOUTHERN METHODIST UNIVERSITY   **Dallas, TX**
Edwin L. Cox School of Business   May 2014

- Candidate for Bachelor of Business Administration
- Concentration in Finance; Minor in History
- Cumulative GPA: 3.7/4.0
- Active Member of the Sigma Chi Fraternity
- Member of Alpha Kappa Psi Business Fraternity
- Member of Alpha Phi Omega Service Fraternity
- Member of the SMU Sailing Club

MAINE SOUTH HIGH SCHOOL   **Park Ridge, IL**
                                                                      May 2007

EXPERIENCE

John Bean Technologies Corporation (NYSE: JBT)   **Chicago, IL**
Summer Intern   May-July 2014

- Worked closely with the Corporate Development team and Accounting Department gaining an understanding for the acquisition and valuation strategies of a global food processing and aero-technology corporation
- Conducted trading comparable analysis on JBT and food processing and aero-technology manufacturing peers. Presented findings to the Corporate Development team and Chief Financial Officer
- Underwent Bloomberg training and developed valuation templates for the Corporate Development team
- Conducted competitor analysis on a key JBT food processing competitor to assess corporate acquisition strategies. Presented findings to the Corporate Development team and Chief Accounting Officer
- Conducted extensive Sarbanes-Oxley compliance testing for the Accounting Department and presented findings to the Chief Accounting Officer

Dearborn Partners LLC   **Chicago, IL**
Summer Intern   *May-July 20137*

- Developed financial knowledge and investment skills at a privately held investment management firm based in Chicago
- Gained experience in analyzing publicly traded companies by creating comprehensive financial models on excel. Models were created by pulling appropriate research from market analysts and examining corporate filings such as the10-K and 10-Q reports, and quarterly conference calls
- Models were created using discounted cash flow valuation to generate the intrinsic value per share of each corporation.
- Assisted directors and managing directors with any necessary office work or research regarding specific companies. Research included overviews of multiple companies 2nd quarter earnings reports, gathering analyst recommendations and thorough searches for current news stories relating to the specified firms
- Met with each managing director of the firm to discuss investment strategies, his or her career path, and received valuable advice for my career going forward and the future of the financial industry as a whole

KELLEY DRYE AND WARREN LLP   **Chicago, IL**
Summer Intern   *June-August 2012*

- Gained an overall knowledge of the corporate attorney lifestyle and responsibilities involved in representing multiple major corporations
- Worked alongside associate attorneys and paralegals to prepare for trials and depositions
- Developed communication and teamwork skills with coworkers in a professional setting
- Gained a knowledge for legal problems faced by many *Fortune 500* companies

SKILLS- Developed expertise using Microsoft Excel, PowerPoint and Bloomberg

David H. Alexander

Xxx Village Fair, #814, Chicago, Illinois, USA, 60060
Mobile: +1-888-999-7156, Email: dalex@gmail.com

PROFILE
Innovative, results oriented executive with demonstrated accomplishments in global general management, marketing, operations, and finance. Expertise includes building teams and enhancing profitability. Groomed over 12 years in the high end consumer products, manufacturing, and leisure industries to lead a multinational division of a Fortune 500 company. Obtained MBA from Kellogg Graduate School of Management.

EDUCATION
KELLOGG SCHOOL OF MANAGEMENT, NORTHWESTERN UNIVERSITY, Evanston, IL
Masters of Business Administration, 2015
BOSTON UNIVERSITY SCHOOL OF MANAGEMENT, Boston, MA
Bachelor of Science in Business Administration (Concentrations: Marketing and Finance), 2003
SEMESTER AT SEA, UNIVERSITY OF PITTSBURGH, Abroad
Itinerary: Asia, Middle East, Eastern Europe, and Northern Africa, 2001

WORK EXPERIENCE
BRUNSWICK CORPORATION
2004-2015
A publicly traded, Fortune 500, company that produces and supplies industry leading recreation products within the marine, fitness, bowling, and billiards industries. Headquartered in Lake Forest, Illinois, Brunswick also participates globally in leisure retailing outlets.

Brunswick Bowling & Billiards, Lake Forest, IL and Hong Kong, China (2004-2010)
Managing Director - Asia Pacific
Boards: Brunswick China Ltd. (Hong Kong) Director, Nippon Brunswick Co. Ltd. (Tokyo) Director

Managed a team of 19 professionals in the fields of sales, marketing, customer support, strategic sourcing, product service and installation, order management, finance, information technology, human resources, and legal at offices in Hong Kong, Shanghai, and Tokyo. Tapped by Division President for this assignment and resided in Hong Kong for three and half years.
- Achieved sales growth of 50% by transitioning regional presence from survival to growth amidst aggressive local competition, traditionally minded, cross cultural and cross functional staff, and a lethargic pool of channel partners, while bridging global communications, fostering company-wide cooperation, and improving the control environment.
- Reorganized regional footprint in order to streamline operations through reductions in force of nearly 80%, function relocation, and unwinding three legal entities.
- Facilitated significant changes in route to market, most notably, in the second largest bowling market in the world, Japan, smoothly and effectively bringing to end a nearly 50 year joint venture with Mitsui Bussan; appointed an independent distributor and established an office for local support.
- Implemented stringent financial controls through disciplined and documented processes and reporting, emphasizing ongoing refinement and transparency, while ensuring consistency with strategic objectives and corporate operating policies, procedures, and guidelines for ethical conduct. Appointed Ethics Counselor.
- Safeguarded competitive presence through product localization, implementation of continuous product training and skills development, intelligence gathering, targeted promotions, legal action, and the aggressive channel management of direct, distributor, and hybrid sales representative force.

Brunswick Bowling & Billiards, Lake Forest, IL   (2001-2004)
Manager of Financial Analysis & Planning
Recruited by the Division CFO, after a year of record losses, to build a new financial and strategic planning department that could halt the performance deficits and guide the organization back to a position that met or exceeded the cost of capital.
- Executed strategic, business planning, pricing, and budgeting processes.
- Provided analysis and support for broad business programs including partnerships, divestitures, new product development, facility relocations, and contract terms and conditions review.
- Supplied management with performance comparisons, insights, and recommendations for corrective action; implemented solutions as appropriate.

Brunswick Corporation, Lake Forest, IL   (2000-2001)
Acquisitions and Business Development Senior Analyst
Board: Advanced Exercise Equipment (Colorado Springs) Director
Secured the position in this small, elite department, reporting to the VP of Business Development, and immediately began supporting the simultaneous divestitures of 10 businesses, representing sales in excess of $700M and involving three investment banks, two accounting firms, two law firms, and various consultants.
- Participated in six equity infusions, two dealer workouts, and one equity investment sale.
- Performed due diligence, market assessment, and investment instrument analysis focusing on options, convertible securities, and equity ownership alternatives, while building and evaluating valuation models.

Brunswick Corporation Financial Leadership Development Program   (1998-2000)
Various Analyst positions in this startup program consisting of national rotations at Brunswick Corporation (Lake Forest, IL), Life Fitness Division (Franklin Park, IL), Brunswick Indoor Recreation Group Division (Lake Forest, IL), and US Marine Division (Arlington, WA).
- Created target and industry portfolios for use in capital market financing, acquisitions, and appropriations.
- Managed various subordinates; documented processes and used them to train three new employees.
- Spearheaded a company-wide employee bowling benefit plan and piloted the Brunswick Outlet e-commerce initiative; Received a Management Award for Excellence.
- Examined boat market share research and analyzed promotional coupon effectiveness at US dealers.
- Completed industrial engineering labor and time standard reassessments for boat production.
- Prepared forward looking planning documents, such as budgets, forecasts, and other ad hoc analysis; partook in the accounting and financial close processes; created historical reporting and audits for management consumption.
- Earned a Best Practice Award for cross-organizational collaboration and continuous improvement.

BURNHAM PARK PLAZA APARTMENTS, Chicago, IL
1997-1998
Independent Market Research Consultant
Contracted by the property owners to perform a market study on available area parking, in order to provide support for valuation claims associated with a move to repurchase the paper on the building from Goldman Sachs. Presentation of findings was provided to all stakeholders and subsequently validated.
- Designed and implemented tenant surveys, observed competitor turnover, benchmarked pricing.
- Researched area development studies and local zoning ordinances and provided site investigations.

ACTIVITIES & SKILLS

Enjoy playing hockey and basketball, listening to live music, and reading historical nonfiction. Proficient in Microsoft Office applications, a Certified Project Manager, and learning to speak Jap

DONALD J. GILCHRIST

CURRENT ADDRESS

Xxx N. Justice Avenue
West Lafayette, IN 47401
(999) 453-7979

HOME ADDRESS

Xxx Sherman Avenue
Evanston, IL 60201
(999) 535-7731

Donald_Gil@gmail.com

CAREER OBJECTIVE

My short-term objective is to seek an entry-level position in the transportation industry, preferably in the operating department of a railroad carrier. My long-term goal is to serve in a supervisory management position related to some aspect of daily ongoing rail freight operations.

EDUCATION

B.B.A., Business Administration Purdue University, West Lafayette, IN - 2004
Major: Transportation
Graduated summa cum laude, GPA 3.8

WORK EXPERIENCE

Summer 2015   Burlington Northern Industries, Chicago
                    Regular Clerk

- Assisted office manager in quality control and general office management areas. Modified office procedures to streamline paper flow, reducing the amount of time spent handling paper by one hour each day.
- Developed new accounts receivable procedure. Improved accounts receivable time by six days.

Summer 2014   AMTRAK, Chicago
                    Porter

- Serviced clients traveling from Chicago to Seattle.
- Developed a system to move baggage from station to client room. Reduced transportation time by 20 percent.

ACTIVITIES AND INTERESTS

- Purdue University Student Railroad Club President and editor of club newspaper.
- Alpha Kappa Alpha Fraternity--held the office of Treasurer and directly responsible for the management of a $200,000 annual budget.
- Purdue University Student Foundation Member--worked as a photographer for the publication and graphics committee.

REFERENCES –Furnished upon request.

Amy L. Smith
Xxx Ottawa Ave
Mt Prospect, IL 60068
(999) 966-9707
amysmith@yahoo.com

QUALIFICATIONS SUMMARY

An elementary education major and math minor that has had nine years of experience in two very highly competitive school districts on the North Shore. Achieved a master's degree in math education. Demonstrated the ability to establish rapport and work exceptionally well with students, parents, fellow teachers and administrators. Recognized as a leader, planner, implementer, and a person who brings out the best in others, especially young people.

EDUCATION

National-Louis University/ M.A. in math education (2001)
DePaul University / B.A. in elementary education with a minor in math

WORK EXPERIENCE

Fall 2008 – present

HIGHCREST MIDDLE SCHOOL – Wilmette, IL
Honors Math Teacher – 5th and 6th grade

Coordinated Placement for math enrichment and honor programs at the 5th and 6th grade level. Designed pretests to determine with 5th grade students would qualify for specific units. Helped a record number of students qualify for high school level math classes in 7th grade.

Fall 2004 – 2008

HIGHCREST MIDDLE SCHOOL – Wilmette, IL
5th Grade Teacher

Taught all subjects including homeroom advisory for five years at the fifth grade level. Worked with gifted, learning disabled and English as a second language students.

Summer 2003 & 2004

SUMMER ENRICHMENT PROGRAM – Wilmette, IL
Math Teacher
Taught both math enrichment and remedial classes to grades 4-8.

Fall 2003 – present

WILMETTER AND KENILWORTH DISTRICTS
Math Tutor

Fall 2002– 2003

JOSEPHS SEARS SCHOOL – Kenilworth, IL
Instructional Assistant
Worked with learning disabled children in grades 5-7.M.

MARGARET O'CONNOR
Xxx West Lake Circle North
Aurora, Colorado 80123
(333) 549-8701
mmargaret@comcast.net

CAREER OBJECTIVE

To obtain a career position in hospital or laboratory administration which will utilize my education and 10 years of technical, clinical, and supervisory experience.

MAJOR ACOMPLISHMENTS

2008 to Present   Supervisor, Hyland Therapeutics Division,
                       Biggs Pharmaceuticals, Inc., Boulder, Colorado

- Directed a staff of nine who worked on 10 major projects during the year. Half of these projects produced a total of $25 million for the company.
- Developed and kept a purchasing and inventory control system. Resulted in staying under department budget by 10 percent or $60,000.
- Directed the conversion of the laboratory from a manual test system to a computerized system. Increased quality control and easy access to vital information.
- Designed and implemented a technical documentation system for the lab. Provided historical data for future research

2004 to 2008   Senior Quality Control Analyst, Hyland Diagnostic Division

- Documented procedures and specifications and interfaced with manufacturing and technical support personnel concerning product problems and special projects.
- Coordinated and supervised the work of four quality control technicians.

2002 to 2004   Quality Control Analyst, Hyland Diagnostic Division

- Tested a varied number of diagnostic product line according to specifications.

2000 to 2002   Little Company of Mary Hospital, Chicago

- Conducted testing in all areas of the clinical laboratory, focusing on critical care.

EDUCATION :

Bachelor of Science, Medical Technology – Loyola University, 2003

The Functional Resume

When your experience is limited but your skills are strong and easily quantified, the functional resume works to your advantage.

The functional resume is often a good choice for an individual who has experienced an employment gap: a displaced homemaker, a person who has taken time out from employment to raise a family, an individual who has been unemployed or unable to work for an extended length of time, and a person whose job was eliminated and must seek alternate employment. The functional resume deemphasizes a person's lack of experience in a job he or she has not yet performed. It is often the best choice for those who are changing careers or leaving one industry for another. The most important thing to remember is, be truthful. You will have to substantiate every item you include in a functional resume.

MICHAEL V. ADAMS: Mike had very little work experience and is a recent college graduate so he emphasized his accomplishments in skill areas important to employers. His intention was to demonstrate that he'd done a lot for his age, and that he has excellent potential.

SUZANNE H. CARLIN: A former teacher, Suzanne is a homemaker who wants to enter the business world. Her reference to a 1000-member organization represents the PTA; the 700-member organization is her church. Suzanne has helped her husband with several small businesses on a part-time basis, and she has developed numerous skills. There is nothing in the resume that is not true. Everything is merely phrased in business terms.

MICHAEL V. ADAMS

CURRENT ADDRESS	HOME ADDRESS

CURRENT ADDRESS

Xxx Forestview Drive
Grinnell, Iowa xxxxx
(700) 555-6710

HOME ADDRESS

Xxx Adams Road
Bloomfield, Michigan xxxxx
Adams@gmail.com

QUALIFICATION SUMMARY

An achievement-oriented liberal arts graduate who has demonstrated the ability to manage and lead others, plan and implement programs, and sell ideas and products.

MAJOR ACCOMPLISHMENTS

Leadership

- Served as President of Tau Kappa Epsilon fraternity, an organization of 50 people. Increased the number of members by 25 percent in one year. Recognized by National as the number-one TKE fraternity for small colleges.
- Directed the Inter-fraternity Council, a governing board of 20 people. Developed a publicity program that increased the number of pledges in system by 10 percent.
- Captained the baseball team which won the All-Iowa Conference baseball title. Made All-Conference and was voted most valuable player.
- Served as a founding member of the Golden Key Club, a national scholastic honorary. Organized all programs during the year.
- Chosen to represent church youth as an elder. Increased the number in the youth group by 30 percent.
- Established Big Brother program linking the Grinnell campus with the community. Held a party on campus twice a year for boys without fathers.

Planning and Implementing Programs

- Organized campus wide vacation program for students. The first year, 100 students signed up for the program.
- Designed and coordinated construction of the fraternity float for homecoming. Won first place.
- Developed an academic support system for students on wing in residence hall, while working as a resident advisor. No one in the group (20 people) obtained below a 2.0 average. Increased overall grade point average from 2.4 to 2.8 (4.0 scale)

177

- Worked with Dean of Students and his staff to rewrite student rules and regulations. The number of infractions was reduced by 15 percent.
- Organized an entrepreneur club on campus. Thirty students learned how to start and operate a successful business.

<u>Selling</u>

- Created a system to sell Columbia music during school year. Took in over 150 orders in one year.
- Conducted a prospecting or cold-calling campaign for a real-estate firm. Produced over 75 potential leads to sales people.
- Captained the debate team in high school that took first in the district and third in the state.
- Served in eight different organizations and sold and implemented over 20 successful new programs.
- Sold programs at all football games. Leading salesperson.

EDUCATION

B.A.   Grinnell College, Grinnell, Iowa, VOIR
          Major: HistoryMinor: Business

          Relevant courses included Introduction to Business, Computer Programming, Accounting, and a sales course offered by Century 21 realty.

HONORS AND ACTIVITIES

- Phi Eta Sigma, national freshman honor society
- Omicron Delta Kappa, national leadership club
- Cardinal XXX, freshman honorary society
- Cardinal Key, sophomore honorary society
- Blue Key, national junior honorary society
- Mortar Board, senior honorary, President
- Computer Club
- Student council representative

REFERENCES

Available upon request.

SUZANNE H. CARLIN
Xxx El Cajon Boulevard
Los Gatos, California xxxxx
(888) 676-3875
SueCarlin@comcast.net

QUALIFICATION SUMMARY

A communications and public relations generalist who has had 20 years of increasing experience and demonstrated achievements in leadership, planning and organization, marketing/promotion, and training.

MAJOR ACCOMPLISHMENTS

Leadership, Planning, Organization

- Directed the operations and public relations area of a 1.2 million dollar business. Lowered complaints by 50 percent the first year.

- Served as President of a 1000-member organization which existed to assist individuals with their educational development. Created a communication system that produced more voluntary help than ever before.

- Worked as part of a team that developed a strategic campaign to elect two local government officials to office. Resulted in landslide victories.

- Elected as one of the directors of a 700-member organization. Headed nominating committee and helped write business plan objectives which were met.

- Served as President of Honors House, Newberry Dorm, and the Sorority Council in college. Enhanced public relations between the student body and administrators.

Marketing/Promotion

- Directed the marketing program of a direct-mail business. Increased sales by 50 percent in one year.

- Coordinated and publicized a yearly event to raise money for charity. Increased profit by 25 percent and cleared over $15,000.

- Developed a marketing program for a national testing program. Signed up 300 customers in two months.

- Created a program that helped the president promote the company. He appeared in newspaper articles five times and on local TV twice within three months. Company's sales increased by 20 percent the first six months.

179

Training/Management

- Headed a communication department. Supervised each member on developing a business plan and evaluated and coached them on their presentation skills. Department received an outstanding evaluation for the year.

- Taught communication skills to over 750 people during a 5-year period. The test scores increased by an average of 3 points.

- Directed 10 organizations over the past 12 years. Improved skills to manage others.

- Managed a group of five for 16 years, with an annual budget ranging from $30,000 to $90,000.

EDUCATION

B.A. Avila College, Kansas City, Missouri

Major: English   Minor: Speech and French

Currently pursuing an M.A. in Marketing Communications from

California State University, Hayward, California

COMMUNITY ACTIVITIES

Montessori School Board – Director (2004 – Present)

Los Gatos Home Owners Association – Secretary (1999 – 2003)

Dryden School Board – President (2002)

Junior League of Los Gatos (1990 - Present)

Community Advisory Committee, Mount Mary College, Program on Women (2003-Present)

Summer Church School - Director (1999)

Avila Alumni Association - Vice President (1995)

El Cajon High School Booster Club Board (2001 - Present)

REFERENCES

Available upon request

The Combination/Creative Resume

This type of resume is often considered "the best of both worlds," since one's skills are featured strongly, but one's work experience is included as well, albeit in a subordinate fashion. Use the combination/creative resume when you want to highlight your strong skills and achievements in a job that wasn't particularly important-looking. Or, if you want to "play down" the industry where you have spent a good deal of time, this type of resume lends itself well.

JACQUELYN B. MIYAKI: Jackie had some very good accomplishments, but a weak employment history. Since the combination/ creative format is indicated by the strength and relevance of employment, it was the right form to use.

DAVID R. ELLIS: Because Dave had many job changes in a three-year period and he did not want to emphasize the furniture industry, he wrote a combination/creative resume. It elicited 15 interviews.

JACQUELYN B. MIYAKI

CURRENT ADDRESS
ADDRESS

Xxx S. Michigan Avenue
Fort Worth, Texas xxxxx
(714) 543-2611
JBMiyaki@comcast.net

HOME

Xxx Seed Street
Waco, Texas xxxxx
(888) 894-1232

QUALIFICATION SUMMARY

An electrical engineering graduate who has demonstrated special research, analytical, and leadership skills.

EDUCATION

B.S.   Texas Christian University, Fort Worth, Texas
Major: Electrical Engineering, June, 2011
GPA: 3.3 overall; 3.5 in major
Special Courses:
Electrical and Electronic Circuits
Electrical Signal Processing
Electromagnetics

MAJOR ACCOMPLISHMENTS

- Participated in a cooperative education program with Motorola, Inc. Created an idea that helped division complete a project that is expected to gross $200 million per year.
- Wrote program for and tutored in the TCU educational technology center. Helped over 100 students in their educational development.
- Worked with a team that developed data acquisition system for monitoring temperature and pressure in the manufacturing process.
- Headed the TCU student union activities program committee. Selected all entertainers who came to campus and coordinated all sound effects for each concert.

HONORS AND AWARDS

- Beta Theta Pi (President-1984)
- Eta Kappa Nu, freshman academic sorority
- Dean's List, seven out of eight semesters
- Phi Eta Sigma
- Omicron Delta Kappa, national leadership society

WORK EXPERIENCE

20014 - 2016	Motorola, Inc., Dallas, Texas
Summer 2013	Camp Counselor, Camp Waldron, Laconia, Louisiana
Summer 2012	Life Guard, Richardson Heights Country Club, Richardson, Texas

David R. Ellis
Xxx Ridgeland Blvd.,
Atlanta, Georgia xxxxx
(888) 869-0351 — Home
(888) 446-9212 — Office
ellis@gmail.com

QUALIFICATIONS

Profit-oriented marketing and planning manager who has demonstrated accomplishments in management, marketing, and strategic planning.

EDUCATION

M.B.A. Marketing	Georgia State University - Atlanta, Georgia - 2010
B.S. Bus. Admin.	University of Georgia - Athens, Georgia - 2004

MAJOR ACCOMPLISHMENTS

Management

- Headed marketing functions of $40 million manufacturing company. Successfully introduced most important new product in company's history on time and within budget. It is generating 15 percent of company's present sales and is projected to account for 40 percent of future profit.
- Developed and directed the marketing program of a $5 million food service company, which generated first profit in two years.
- Founded and coordinated advertising and promotion department for a broadcast subsidiary of American Broadcasting Companies, Inc. (ABC). Organization maintained its threatened number-two position in volatile marketplace.
- Directed marketing and sales staff in southeast region. Increased market share by 40 percent within one year with increase in profit margin.
- Organized and conducted training program for sales force and dealer network which increased product selling effectiveness.
- Unified and headed engineering, manufacturing, and marketing in speeding up development of a crucial product and launching it.

Marketing

- Conducted competitive analysis which uncovered pricing disadvantages. Recommended and implemented strategy which realigned pricing structure and resulted in 125 percent growth within 1 1/2 years.
- Formulated and implemented reorganization of distribution channels. Increased sales by 25 percent, along with improved dealer relationships.
- Supervised media campaign which helped firm increase market share in competitive marketplace.

183

- Originated new corporate identification program as part of successful company revitalization.
- Analyzed needs for Fortune 100 Company, then personally sold major purchasing agreement after three other members of senior management had failed to gain contract.

Strategic Planning

- Spearheaded corporate opportunity analysis. Resulted in successful $3 million investment.
- Developed and conducted market research study, which uncovered profitable market niches in fastest growing segment of industry.
- As manager of marketing and planning, conducted financial analysis recommending elimination of two developmental products. Saved company approximately $300,000.
- Headed product line planning for company's largest product segment. These products increased volume by 30 percent over two years.

PROFESSIONAL HISTORY

2001 to present	SOUTHERN BELLE CORPORATION — Atlanta, Georgia District Manager Marketing Manager — Systems Product Development Territory Sales Manager Manager — Marketing Development Marketing Manager — Seating
2000 - 2001	REBEL MANUFACTURING — Americus, Georgia Manager — Marketing and Planning
1997 – 1999	WKQZ RADIO - Marietta, Georgia (subsidiary of American Broadcasting Companies, Inc.)[19] Advertising and Promotion Director
1995 – 1997	ROMA'S OF GEORGIA — Athens, Georgia Marketing Director

HONORS AND AWARDS

- Received creative award for advertisement on systems furniture (2003).
- Authored article entitled "Practical Constraints to Idealized Market Research," Proceedings of Southern Marketing Association (2000)
- Editor-in-Chief of campus newspaper (1995)

REFERENCES- Available Upon Request

APPENDIX C
SAMPLE LETTERS

SAMPLE LETTERS

You have to develop and send letters as part of your job search campaign.
We have enclosed five sample letters that can you create as you conduct your job search campaign.

1) Networking letters.

2) Answering print or online ads

3) Direct letters to the hiring executives in companies

4) Search firm letters

5) Broadcast letters

Network Letters-Selling and Instructing Your Network

Before most people will assist you, they must believe in you and know how they can help. The majority of people you contact are not career counselors. Therefore, you must approach them with confidence, a career goal, and a plan of action to keep your name in their minds. It sells you and makes your contacts feel more comfortable. Listed on the following pages are five net working letters. Read each over and develop your letters based on how you want to work with people in your network.

Networking Letter A
Xxx Keystone Avenue
Park Forest, AL xxxxx

Mrs. Louise Hernandez   Date
Burns Industries, Inc.
Xxxx West Lincoln Ave.
Birmingham, AL xxxxx

Dear Louise,

I am writing to ask your help in my job search. As you know, I have been with X.Y.Z. Company for the past eight years and have enjoyed good progress with them. Now due to reorganization and a reduction in force, my position has been eliminated.

I plan to call you in the near future to tell you more about my situation. In the meantime, I am enclosing a copy of my resume which outlines my background employment history, and accomplishments. My objective is to continue in _____...

 I would appreciate your assistance in:

> - Alerting me to any potential job openings which match my qualifications
> - Supplying me names and phone numbers of people who may know of potential jobs

Thank you in advance for your time and assistance. If you are aware of any current opening, please call me before I call you.

Sincerely,

 Jane C. Harkness

Networking Letter B

Xxx Harton Rd.
Milwaukee, WI xxxxx

Mr. Jack Harris   Date
Xxx Spruce Lane
Mequon, WI xxxxx

Dear Jack,

I want to thank you for your suggestions and the time you took listening to me talk about my job search. As I stated on the telephone, I am looking for a position as a _____ in the _____ industry. My resume is enclosed for your review.

I appreciated your giving me the job lead with ABC Company and list of people to contact. If you should hear about other job openings or about other people to contact, please let me know.

Thanks again.

Sincerely,

Ronald T. Brown

Networking Letter C
(Written by a recent college grad)

Xxx Jones Rd.
Green Bay, Wisconsin xxxxx

June 1, 2011

Mr. Irving J. Sawtell
Xxxx Escanaba Avenue
Flint, MI xxxxx
May 15, 2011

Dear Mr. Sawtell:

I am writing to ask your help in my job search. As you know, I am a marketing major at Michigan State University and will graduate in June.

My short range career objective is to find an entry level position in marketing. Enclosed is a copy of my resume that outlines my background and achievements.

I plan to call you in the near future to tell you more about my situation. I would appreciate your assistance in:

- Alerting me to any potential job openings
- Supplying me names and phone numbers of people who may know of potential marketing jobs.
- Using your name to obtain an informational interview when I call them.

Thank you.

Sincerely,
Leslie C. Burns

188

Networking Letter D
(a homemaker reentering job market)
Xxx North Franklin
San Francisco, CA xxxxx

Mr. John H. Dennison   Date
IBM Corporation
Xxx Commonwealth Blvd.
Menlo Park, CA xxxxx

Dear Jack,

I am writing to ask your help with my job search. After many years as a manager of a family, I have decided to transfer my skills and find employment with a company or organization.

My short range goal is to achieve an entry level position in _____. Enclosed is a copy of my resume that outlines my skills, education, and work experience. I would appreciate your alerting me to any potential job openings or supplying me names and phone numbers of people who may know of potential jobs in this area.

I plan to call you in the near future to learn about any ideas or suggestions you might have to help me. Thank you in advance for your time.

Sincerely,

Carla Eddleston

Networking Letter E
Xxxx College Avenue
Bismark, ND xxxxx

Mr. Jack Sawtell   Date
Acme Resins Corporation
Xxx Westling Road
Fargo, ND xxxxx

Dear Jack (or Dear Mr. Sawtell, depending on your relationship),

Attached is a list of companies that I would like to approach about a position in
_____. At a convenient time, I would appreciate your reviewing the list and
writing in the names of the people you know that work for these companies. Their title,
telephone number and e-mail would be extremely helpful to me..

 If you can think of other companies and their employees, please add them to the list. I
would like to use your name when I call them. So you feel more comfortable when
I call them, I would like to go over the list of people and review with you what I am going to
say to them. I want to make sure I come across in a positive way.

Since my goal is to contact these executives as soon as possible, your response to when we
might talk would be deeply appreciated. Thank you ahead of time for your assistance.

Sincerely,

George G. Thompson

SPECIAL NOTE: if you want the names of people who work for search firms,
 private equity and venture capital groups, you might also ask for that information in
 the letter.

Networking Letter F
Xxx Sanderson Circle
Anaheim, CA xxxxx

Ms. Barbara Kujimoto   Date
Towne Applied Technology, Inc.
Xxx Howard Street
New York, NY xxxxx

Dear Barb,

Enclosed, for your consideration, is a copy of George E. Smith's resume, which I recently received from him. I have worked with George on a number of special projects during the past few years with good results. He has always done a fine job representing his employer and is extremely dependable.

I recommend him highly.

Sincerely,

Ronald C. Molinaro

Networking Letter G
Xxx Riverside Drive
Portsmouth, MA xxxxx

Ms. Karen Conway   Date
Bullock Associates
Xxx Freedom Parkway
Bangor, ME xxxxx

Dear Ms. Conway,

A common acquaintance of ours, <u>Alicia Von Pelt</u>, has suggested that I contact you in regard to
my job search as a _____.

My professional background demonstrates an excellent record of accomplishments in operations
management, and a wide range of responsibilities in both technical and general management.
Key among these are significant achievements in advanced manufacturing technologies,
operations management, and planning. I have been able to improve utilization of both people and
facilities while reducing costs and increasing efficiency and quality.

I view myself as both a team unit leader and a team player. Over the years, I have developed a
talent and performance management system that has worked for me in transforming direct
reports and my unit into top performers.

A copy of my resume is attached for your perusal. I would like to call you in the near future to
learn if you might have some time to meet with me.

Sincerely,

Michael C. Sullivan
Encl.

Networking Letter H
(recent college grad)
Xxxx West 111th Street
St. Louis, Missouri xxxxx

Mr. Bart Weed   Date
First National Bank of St. Louis
Xxx West 77th Place
St. Louis, Missouri xxxxx

Dear Mr. Weed:

At the suggestion of Richard Johnson, I am writing to learn about the possibility of meeting you. I am a finance major at the University of Missouri and will be graduating in June. My career objective is to work in the banking industry and I thought you might share some of your banking experience with me.

I will call you within a few weeks. Any time you might give me would be deeply appreciated. My time is flexible.

Sincerely,

Sheila L. Lindsey

Website and Ad Letters

LINDA K. FANNELLI
Xxxxx South Hamilton
Country Club Hills, Illinois xxxxx
(999) 555-4444
lkfannelli@hotmail.com

Date

Director, Human Resources
Delta Corporation
Xx N. Michigan Avenue
Chicago, Illinois xxxxx

Dear Sir:

Your ad from the website found on Monster.com for a computer programmer appears to match my background and capabilities. Enclosed is a copy of my resume. Some of my skills and recent accomplishments include the following:

- Developed programming skills in BASIC, RPG, COBOL, and BASIC Assembly Language.

- As a computer lab aide, coordinated and debugged over 175 programs.

- Taught the operational procedures of the IBM systems to 300 people.

- Maintained a filing system for all programs, which reduced theft by 50 percent.

- Operated card readers and keypunch machine.

- Developed a system to monitor inventory supplies. Reduced costs by five percent.

I received an A.A.S. in computer programming from Triton College in 2010.

I will be happy to discuss further details with you in a personal interview.

Sincerely,

Enclosure

Specific Cover Letter (Blind Ad)

M. MARGARET O'CONNOR
Xxx West Lake Circle North
Aurora, Colorado xxxx
(999) 549-8701
mmargaret@sbcglobal.net

Date

Dear Sir/Madame:

In response to your ad on *Career Builder* for a laboratory supervisory position, I have enclosed my resume for your review.

My technical, clinical, and supervisory experience appear to be very good match to you ad. Listed below are some of my accomplishments which have helped me progress in my career:

- Directed a staff of nine that developed projects which generated $25 million dollars in one year.

- Designed a purchasing and inventory system that saved $60,000.

- Converted the laboratory from a manual test system to a computerized system.

I will be happy to discuss further details of my experience with you in a personal interview.

Sincerely,

Enclosure

Direct Letter to a Company (Controlled Blitz)

Jack Smith
CEO and President
ABC Company
Xxx Skokie Blvd.
Northbrook, Illinois xxxxx

Dear Jack,

The difference many times between a company being great rather than average is leadership. You might have a need to add a seasoned executive such as myself to your senior management team to help your company become more efficient and effective.

My career path includes working 35 years for a major multi- line insurance company in the following positions.

- Senior Vice President and Chief Life Actuary
- CEO and President of a small subsidiary
- Senior Vice President and Chief Investment Operations Officer
- Operations Review Officer
- Product Development and Pricing

I have a proven track record in helping organizations increase profit by making internal operations more efficient and effective. I could head up one or a number of functional areas for you such as administration, finance, audit, and human resources plus help you develop and execute a solid business plan.

I have a M.S. and B.A. from Northwestern University in Evanston, Illinois. I will call you in a few days and see if we can meet and discuss how we could be of mutual benefit to each other. Thanks for your time.

Lew Jackson

Search Firm Letters

ALFRED J. DOBBS
Xxx Harper's Ferry Rd.
Bridgeport, CN xxxxx
(999) 567-1212
Dobbs123@gmail.com

Date

Mr. Michael Jones
Williston & Associates
Xx Landmark Square
Stamford, Connecticut xxxxx

Dear Mr. Jones:

Enclosed is my resume for consideration against your client assignments. My professional background demonstrates significant accomplishments in:

- operations management
- business and strategic planning
- budget and cost controls

My experience includes progressively increasing responsibilities with Fortune 500 companies in both domestic and international businesses. Since your agency also works internationally, I might emphasize my experience in this area.

My career objective is general management, which may be achieved through an operations or planning position. My base salary is $100,000 with a bonus of $50,000.

I will be happy to discuss my background in greater detail. Please feel free to contact me at the above number to set up a mutually convenient appointment.

Sincerely,

Enclosure

<u>Search-Firm Letter</u> (Update)

DAVID R. ELLIS
Xxx Ridgeland Blvd.
Atlanta, GA xxxxx
(999) 869-0351
drellis@comcast.net

Date

Ms. Elizabeth Smith
VEW Search, Inc.
Xx Broadway
New York, New York xxxxx

Dear Ms. Smith:

I am writing to provide a status report on my job search activities since contacting you in February, 2006.

Several opportunities have been reviewed, ranging from "very exciting" to "no fit." Out of 15 candidates interviewed by a search firm, I was one of the final two people interviewed by the Executive Vice-President for the Vice-President of Marketing position. The other candidate, who is currently Vice-President of Marketing for a Fortune 500 company, was selected. I have turned down one offer that did not fit.

As the New Year starts, I would appreciate your continuing interest and consideration concerning client assignments you are handling.

Sincerely,

Search-Firm Letter (Following Telephone Interview)

PAUL H. GOLDBERG
Xxx Canterbury Place
Brookdale, MA xxxxx
(999) 356-1867
phgoldber@gmail.com
Date

Mr. Edward Smith
ABC Search Company
Xx Park Plaza
New York, New York xxxxx

Dear Mr. Smith:

Since your client is seeking a marketing manager with experience in construction products, my qualifications will certainly be of interest to you. I believe the combination of my corporate exposure and line experience would enable me to make a profitable contribution to both short- and long-term market strategies.

As Manager of Strategic Planning, I am responsible for the strategic direction and profit improvement of an $800 million operating group. Some of my past accomplishments include the following:

- Planned, organized and conducted strategic analysis of company's largest facility. Recommendations resulted in product consolidation, expansion and cost reduction investments that will generate a $40-$50 million profit turnaround upon full implementation.
- Conducted product/market productivity improvement program for specialty millwork operation. Recommended shift in product mix that resulted in 15 percent increase in profitability.
- Refocused marketing and distribution program of high-quality product that led to doubling of capacity.
- Held P&L responsibility on multimillion-dollar capital equipment contracts for industrial and utility customers. Effectively managed all phases from proposal to start-up. Negotiated scope, price, and performance guarantees with customers and suppliers.

I am enclosing a resume for your perusal. I hope you find my background compatible with your management needs and that I may meet with you to elaborate on my accomplishments. I look forward to hearing from you regarding this possibility.

Sincerely,

Enclosure

Broadcast Letters

The broadcast letter can stand without a resume, although it doesn't have to be sent alone. The broadcast letter arrives unsolicited; that is, the company receiving the letter may not have a job opening at all. The letter's purpose is to pique the reader's curiosity and to interest him or her in you as a job candidate. Hence, this letter must be written creatively or not at all.

Broadcast Letter (Without Resume)

MICHAEL V. ADAMS
Xxx Southfield Road
Bloomfield, Michigan xxxxx
(999) 678-0210
Adams_michael@yahoo.com

Date

Mr. Joseph Hobbs
Vice President of Human Resources
J. Briscoe, Inc.
Xx Elm Street
Grand Rapids, Michigan xxxxx

Dear Mr. Hobbs:

A recent survey by the American Management Association of Chief Executive Officers in 5000 U.S. corporations revealed a need to achieve results and the ability to work with a wide variety of people as the top two reasons for their success.

Your company might be interested in talking to a recent liberal arts graduate who has this need and ability to achieve results.

My career goal is to begin working in a sales position and then progress toward an executive position. Some of my key accomplishments include:

- Served as President of an organization of 50 people. Increased membership by 25 percent in one year.
- Developed an academic support system for 20 people. Increased the group grade point average from 2.4 to 2.8 (4.0 scale) in one year. No one received less than a C average.
- Created a system to sell cell phones during school year. I took in over 150 orders.
- Participated in a summer cold-calling program for a real estate firm, producing 75 leads for the sales people.

I would like to have the opportunity to meet with you. I will call you in the next few days to learn when we might be able to get together.

Sincerely

Broadcast Letter (Without Resume)

JACQUELYN B. MIYAKI
Xxx Seed Street
Waco, Texas xxxxx
(999) 894-1232
jbmiyaki@mail.com

Date

Mr. Robert C. Pace
Vice-President of Engineering
Texas Electronics, Inc.
Xxx Yellow Rose Highway
Houston, TX xxxxx

Dear Mr. Pace:

You may be interested in an electrical engineer who worked part-time and helped a Fortune 100 company complete a project that will generate an expected $200 million in sales next year.

I will be graduating from Texas Christian University this June with a B.S. in Electrical Engineering. Some of my achievements include these:

— Writing programs for and tutoring students in the educational technology center.

— Working with a team that developed data acquisitions systems for monitoring temperature and pressure in the manufacturing process.

— Participating in a cooperative education program with Motorola, Inc.

— Coordinating all sound effects for concerts on campus.

— Serving as President of Omicron Delta Kappa, a national leadership organization.

I will be happy to discuss further details of my experience with you in a personal interview. I plan to call you in the near future to learn when we might be able to meet.

Sincerely,

Appendix C
105 Fastest-Growing Franchises*
*As reported in the February 2014 issue of *Entrepreneur* magazine[17]

7-Eleven Inc.
Convenience store
Total Franchises: 32,701
(800) 255-0711

Aaron's Sales & Lease
Ownership
Furniture, electronics, computer
& appliance leasing & sales
Total Franchises: 510
(678) 402-3778

Ace Hardware Corp.
Hardware & home improvement
store
Total Franchises: 4,693
(630) 990-6900

Aire Serv Heating & Air
Conditioning Inc.
Heating, ventilation & air
conditioning services
Total Franchises: 180
(800) 583-2662

Allegra network
Printing center
Total Franchises: 423
(248) 596-8600

ampm Mini Market
Convenience store & gas station
Total Franchises: 2,700
(888) 894-2676

Anago Cleaning Systems
Commercial cleaning
Total Franchises: 1,233
(800) 213-5857

Anytime Fitness
Fitness center
Total Franchises: 782
(800) 704-5004

Arby's
Sandwiches, chicken, salads
Total Franchises: 2,558
(678) 514-4100

Aussie Pet Mobile
Mobile pet grooming
Total Franchises: 548
Auntie Anne's Hand-Rolled Soft
Pretzels
Hand-rolled soft pretzels
Total Franchises: 942
(717) 435-1479

Baby Boot Camp
Prenatal & postnatal fitness
Total Franchises: 118
(888) 990-2229

Bark Busters Home Dog
Training
In-home dog training
Total Franchises: 366
(877) 300-2275

Batteries Plus
Batteries & related products
Total Franchises: 315
(800) 274-9155

Baymont Inn & Suites
Hotels
Total Franchises: 210
(800) 758-8999

Bonus Building Care
Commercial cleaning
Total Franchises: 2,119
(800) 931-1102

Boston Pizza Restaurants LP
Casual dining restaurant &
sports bar
Total Franchises: 352
(866) 277-8721

Buffalo Wild Wings
Buffalo wings & sandwiches
Total Franchises: 351
(800) 499-9586

Camp Bow Wow
Dog day care & boarding
services
Total Franchises: 81
(877) 700-2275

Carl's Jr. Restaurants
Hamburgers
Total Franchises: 763
(866) 253-7655

Cartridge World
Printer/fax cartridge
replacements & sales
Total Franchises: 1,696
(510) 594-9900

CertaPro Painters Ltd.
Residential & commercial
painting
Total Franchises: 439
(800) 462-3782

Charley's Grilled Subs
Philly cheese steaks, grilled
subs, fries, salads
Total Franchises: 329
(800) 437-8325

Chester's Int'l.
Quick-service chicken restaurant
Total Franchises: 82
(800) 646-9403

Choice Hotels Int'l
Hotels, inns, suites, resorts
Total Franchises: 5,709
(866) 560-9871

Coffee News
Weekly newspaper distributed at
restaurants
Total Franchises: 1,142
(207) 941-0860

Colbert/Ball Tax Service
Tax preparation & electronic
filing
Total Franchises: 322
(713) 592-5555

Cruise Planners Franchising
LLC/American Express
Cruise/tour travel agency
Total Franchises: 766
(888) 582-2150

CruiseOne Inc.
Cruise travel agency
Total Franchises: 549
(800) 892-3928

Denny's Inc.
Full-service family restaurant
Total Franchises: 1,191
(800) 304-0222

Domino's Pizza LLC
Pizza, breadsticks, buffalo wings
Total Franchises: 8,053
(734) 930-3030

Ductz Int'l. Inc.
Duct & vent cleaning
Total Franchises: 113
(877) 382-8987

Dunkin Donuts
Coffee, doughnuts, baked goods
Total Franchises: 8,082
(561) 626-4114

Edible Arrangements Int'l. Inc.
Floral –like designs from
sculpted fresh fruit
Total Franchises: 750
(888) 727-4258

Elements Therapeutic Massage
Inc.
Therapeutic massage studio
Total Franchises: 52
(303) 663-0880
El Pollo Loco
Flame-grilled chicken meals &
Mexican entrees
Total Franchises: 245
(714) 599-5000

Expense Reduction analysts
Cost-reduction consulting
Total Franchises: 206
(760) 712_ 3607

Express Tax
Tax preparation & electronic
filing
Total Franchises: 647
(888) 417-4461

Fast-teks On-site Computer
Services
On-site computer repair services
Total Franchises: 183
(800) 262-1671
Firehouse Subs
Submarine sandwiches
Total Franchises: 310
(904) 886-8300

Fitness Together
Personal fitness training
Total Franchises: 409
(303) 663-0880

Five Star Painting
Residential & commercial
painting
Total Franchises: 68
(801) 804-6677

Great Clips Inc.
Hair salon
Total Franchises: 2,688
(800) 999-5959

Goddard Systems Inc.
Preschool/child-care center
Total Franchises: 297
(800) 272-4901

Goin' Postal
Retail shipping & business
services
Total Franchises: 297
(813) 782-1500
Hampton Inn/Hampton Inn &
suites
Mid-price hotels
Total Franchises: 1,534
(800) 286-0645

Hardee's
Burgers, chicken, biscuits
Total Franchises: 1,397
(866) 253-7655

Health Source Chiropractic and
Progressive Rehab.
Chiropractic, nutrition &
weight-loss services
Total Franchises: 195
(440) 967-5458
Hilton Garden Inn
Upscale mid-price hotels
Total Franchises: 368
(800) 286-0645

Home Helpers/Direct Link
Nonmedical care services
Total Franchises: 750
(800) 216-4196

Homewood Suites by Hilton
Upscale extended-stay hotels
Total Franchises: 196
(800) 286-0645

Instant Tax Service
Retail tax prep. & electronic
filing
Total Franchises: 1,181
(888) 870-1040

Inter Continental Hotels Group
Hotels
Total Franchises: 3,498
(770) 604-2000
Jan-Pro Franchising Intl'. Inc.
Commercial cleaning
Total Franchises: 8,875
(678) 336-1780

Jani-King
Commercial cleaning
Total Franchises: 12,980
(800) 552-5264

Jantize American
Commercial cleaning
Total Franchises: 110
(888) 540-0001

Jazzercise Inc.
Dance/exercise classes
Total Franchises: 7,578
(760) 476-1750

Jiffy Lube Int'l. Inc.
Fast oil change
Total Franchises: 2,001
(800) 327-9532

Jimmy John's Gourmet
Sandwich Shops
Gourmet sandwiches
Total Franchises: 701
(800) 546-6904

Knights Franchise Systems
Hotels
Total Franchises: 290
(800) 758-8999

LA Boxing Franchise Corp.
Cardio boxing & kickboxing
classes
Total Franchises: 115
(866) 522-6946

La Quinta Franchising LLC
Hotels
Total Franchises: 294
(214) 492-6600

Lenny's Sub Shop
Philly cheese steaks & sub
sandwiches
Total Franchises: 168
(901) 753-4002

Liberty Tax Service
Income-tax preparation
Total Franchises: 2,579
(800) 790-3863

Long John Silver's Restaurants
Inc.
Fish & chicken
Total Franchises: 791
(866) 298-6986

Massage Envy
Therapeutic massage services
Total Franchises: 457
(602) 889-1090

McDonald's
Hamburgers, chicken, salads
Total Franchises: 24,799
(630) 623-6196

Mint Condition Franchising Inc.
Janitorial & building
maintenance services
Total Franchises: 110
(803) 548-6121

MonitorClosely.com
Digital surveillance systems
Total Franchises: 120
(800) 797-7505

Monthly Coupons
Direct-mail advertising
Total Franchises: 45
(909) 386-0550

Mr. Handyman Int'l. LLC
Home maintenance & repairs
Total Franchises: 315
(800) 289-4600

Mr. Sandless Inc.
Sandless wood floor refinishing
Total Franchises: 89
(610) 364-2080

Nrgize Lifestyle Café
Smoothies, meal-replacement
shakes, protein bars
Total Franchises: 68
(480) 362-4800

PaPa John's Int'l. Inc.
Pizza
Total Franchises: 2,615
(502) 261-7272

PaPa Murphy's
Take-and-bake pizza
Total Franchises: 1,006
(360) 260-7272

Pet Butler
Pet waste cleanup & removal
Total Franchises: 132
(800) 738-2885

Philly Pretzel Factory
Pretzel bakery
Total Franchises: 101
(800) 679-4221

Pizza Hut
Pizza
Total Franchises: 10,239
(866) 298-6986

Planet Beach Franchising Corp.
Spa & UV-treatment services
Total Franchises: 393
(888) 290-8266

Planet Fitness
Fitness club
Total Franchises: 209
(603) 750-0001

Play N Trade Franchise Inc.
New & used video games
Total Franchises: 178
(888) 768-4263

Pretzelmaker/Pretzel Time
Gourmet pretzels
Total Franchises: 279
(800) 524-6444

Puroclean
Insurance restoration services
Total Franchises: 224
(800) 775-7876

Qdoba Mexican Grill
Fast-casual Mexican food
Total Franchises: 334
(720) 898-2300

Right at Home Inc.
Senior home care & medical
staffing
Total Franchises: 150
(877) 697-7537

Rita's Italian Ice
Italian ices, frozen custard,
gelati
Total Franchises: 521
(800) 677-7482

Robeks Fruit Smoothies &
Healthy Eats
Fruit smoothies & healthy foods
Total Franchises: 162
(866) 476-2357

Roni Deutch Tax Center
Tax preparation & business
services
Total Franchises: 44
(866) 738-2289

Rooter-Man
Plumbing, drain & sewer
cleaning
Total Franchises: 462

(800) 700-8062
Senior Helpers
Home care for seniors
Total Franchises: 152
(800) 760-6389

Servpro
Insurance/disaster restoration &
cleaning
Total Franchises: 1,420
(800) 826-9586

Snap Fitness Inc.
24 hour fitness center
Total Franchises: 701
(952) 474-5422

Sonic Drive In Restaurants
Drive-in restaurant
Total Franchises: 2,768
(800) 569-6656

Sport Clips
Men's sports-themed hair salon
Total Franchises: 563
(512) 869-1201

Smoothie King
Smoothies & healthy products
Total Franchises: 563
(800) 577-4200

Stratus Building Solutions
Commercial cleaning
Total Franchises: 1,339
(314) 731-2000

Stroller Strides LLC
Stroller fitness program
Total Franchises: 260
(866) 348-4666

Subway
Sub sandwiches & salads
Total Franchises: 29,612
(800) 888-4848

System4
Commercial cleaning
Total Franchises: 704
(216) 524-6100

The Maids Home Service
Residential cleaning
Total Franchises: 1,033
(800) 843-6243

Value Place
Extended-stay hotel
Total Franchises: 69
(888) 456-8737

Vanguard Cleaning Systems
Commercial cleaning
Total Franchises: 1,175
(800) 564-6422

Visiting Angels
Non medical home-care services
Total Franchises: 334
(800) 365-4189

Wingstop Restaurants Inc.
Chicken wings
Total Franchises: 341
(972) 686-6500

Wireless Zone
Wireless communications store
Total Franchises: 287
(860) 632-9494

Appendix D
Bibliography

1. Wesley Habley, Jennifer Bloom and Steve Robbins. *Student Graduation Trends from 1983 to 2014*. American College Testing Program, 2012. Page 2.

2. Noel and Levitz. *Why Am I Here?* 2012. Page 3

3. The *2015 ACT National Norms Report*, American College Testing Program. Page 4

4. *Binge Drinking*. National Center on Alcohol and Substance Abuse Study, 1993-2014. Page 6

5. Gardner, P. 2010-2014 Recruiting Trends Report. Career Services Department and Collegiate Employment Research Institute. Michigan State University, East Lansing, Michigan. Page 7

6. Habley and McClananhan. *What works in Student Retention*, 2014. American College Testing Program. Page 11

7. Daniel Goleman. *Working with Emotional Intelligence*. Bantam Books,1998. Page 50

8. *Average Yearly Salaries of Workers Ages 18 and Older*, The U.S. Census Bureau, 2014, Page. 78

9. *Breakdown of Household Income in America*. The U.S. Census Bureau, 2014, p. 17. Page 78

10. *Median Age of Males and Females Marrying*-A 30 Year Study-1970 to 2010, U.S Census Bureau, Page 80.

11. *Motivation of Workers,* Frederick Herzberg, 1998, Page 81

12. Execunet's 2014 Annual Executive Job Market Report, *Average Executive Tenure. Page 81*

13..*Average CEO Time in a Job*, Chicago Tribune, June, 2013, Page 91

14. Ten Career Groups and Related Positions, *Enhanced Occupational Outlook Handbook,* 2014, Page 101

15. *Top 115 Projected Career Positions Until 2014*, U.S. Department of Labor. Page 109.

16. Majors/Related Careers, ACT Registration Form, 2014. Page 112

17. 105 Fastest Growing Franchises. February 2012, Issue of *Entrepreneur Magazine*

Something to Remember
-Graduating from College with a Good Job and Future-

Poem

If you think you are beaten, you are,
If you think you dare not, you don't.
If you like to win, but you think you can't,
It is almost certain you won't.

If you think you'll lose, you're lost
For out of the world we find,
Success begins with a person's will-
It's all in the state of mind.

If you think you are outclassed, you are,
You got to think high to rise,
You've got to be sure of yourself before
You can ever win a prize.

Life battles don't always go
To the stronger or faster person.
But soon or later the person who wins
Is the person who think he/she can."

Quote-Achievement Motivation Program
Clement Stone Foundation

Author, Career Consultant and Speaker
Michael V. Mulligan, Ph.D.

Dr. Mulligan has spent much of his career and life *helping* people find direction in their lives as well as new jobs. He prepared for his career by obtaining a Ph.D. in counseling from the University of Georgia, an M.A. in counseling and student personnel work in higher education from Michigan State University and a B.A. in liberal arts from Alma College.

Dr. Mulligan presently directs and owns Mulligan Associates, Inc., a 32 year career and talent management consulting firm that has helped over 10,000 individuals with career direction and finding new positions. This has included CEOs, Presidents, Chief Level Officers, partners from consulting firms, senior executives, managers, professionals, nonexempt workers and college students majoring in different subjects from various colleges and universities across the United States.

Dr. Mulligan has served as a *fellow manager* with the International Career Certification Institute. The Institute certifies people in the career management consulting field. Fellow Managers assist in checking out the credentials and experience of those applying for certification. Dr. Mulligan wrote an article *What it Takes to Be an Effective Career Consultant* and it has been a guide for the industry for the last 20 years.

Prior to starting Mulligan & Associates Inc., Dr. Mulligan worked as Management Development Director for Century 21 of Northern Illinois. He and the six consultants that reported to him worked with over 400 owners and 700 office managers of Century 21 franchises to help them develop plans, hire the right people and grow the business.

Before Century 21, Dr. Mulligan was the Regional Director for the American College Testing Program servicing state departments, high schools and colleges in five mid western states. He worked closely with educators teaching them how to use ACT score reports and data to help students grow, select the right major and career and graduate from college.

Prior to ACT, Dr. Mulligan worked as Director of Orientation and Assistant Director of Admissions at the University of Georgia. He coordinated 150 student/parent orientation sessions, met with over 30 high school and community college students weekly to help them decide if the University of Georgia was right for them and gave over 500 college night speeches. He also served as the Chairman of the Georgia High School/ College Articulation Committee for three years. This committee established the state-wide college night programs and other programs to help high school students make post-secondary plans.

Before the University of Georgia, Dr. Mulligan served as a counselor in the counseling center at Georgia Tech. He worked with over 600 students helping them decide on a college major and how to stay in school. Much of his work focused on helping students with personal issues which impacted their staying or leaving school.

209

Printed in the United States
by Baker & Taylor Publisher Services